The Open Schoolhouse

Building a Technology Program to
Transform Learning and Empower Students

Charlie Reisinger

The Open Schoolhouse
Building a Technology Program to Transform Learning and Empower Students

http://theopenschoolhouse.com
@OpenSchoolhouse

Copyright © 2016 Charlie Reisinger

This work is licensed under a Creative Commons Attribution-NonCommercial-ShareAlike 4.0 International License.

Cover Design by Zach LeBar

ISBN: 1537484052
ISBN-13: 978-1537484051
First Printing October 2016

For past, present, and future students.

Contents

	Introduction	1
1	A Brief Open Source Lesson	5
2	Beginnings and Foundations	17
3	An Open Technology Team	35
4	Linux is Elementary	45
5	Planning a One-to-One Program	61
6	Student Apprentices	77
7	Building the One-to-One Program	91
8	High School Laptops Launch	109
9	The Power of Open	119
	Epilogue	137
	Appendix: Software Resources	139
	Acknowledgements	143
	About Penn Manor School District	145
	About the Author	147
	Notes	149

Introduction

To best prepare students for the future, we must think deeply and openly about our vision for school technology today. I believe every student, in every school, deserves equal and open access to computers. Students should have the freedom to explore and experiment with their school-issued devices. In an open schoolhouse, every student is trusted with powerful learning technology and empowered to rewire and reshape the world.

For many public schools, fiscal nightmares disrupt student technology dreams. An escalating multi-year budget crisis has pulverized education budgets in my home state of Pennsylvania. The scenario is similar in many states and countries. While legislators bicker over the politics of a spending plan, public schools struggle with inadequate funding and growing student needs.

Technology purchase and support costs are pain points for school directors. Reliable technology infrastructure is as vital as electricity and plumbing, but these services are not cheap. Schools must also wrestle ongoing, yearly software costs. From classroom software to school-wide learning programs, the price of costly commercial software can choke school budgets.

Worse than a scarcity of affordable technology is technology that's locked down to young minds. School administrators often implement draconian restrictions on classroom computers. Students may not install software, examine code, or tinker with the underlying operating system. Restricted devices run only the apps and software school administrators say should run. Programming is out of reach, as if under glass.

It's hard to understand this closed attitude toward education—students are handed powerful learning devices and instructed not to lift the hood, not to explore what makes the device work, not to learn about computing. What can a student learn from a computer or tablet purposely configured to stop exploration? With the command line off-limits and programming tools sequestered, students become puppets on someone else's code string.

Locked-down technology is a symptom of an education model designed for student compliance and defined by the incessant measurement of learning. A factory-like school system values what a student has purportedly learned on a linear path, as demonstrated by a standardized test score. Technology device restraints and restrictions lock students on the assessment assembly line, at the cost of a child's curiosity and intellectual freedom. Computers were once the spark for a child's imagination. Now, they are a testing apparatus for assessment monarchs.

We must challenge those who believe computers exist solely for testing, Googling, and as electronic worksheets. Computer technology is powerful because it enables students to learn by building and creating. Tapping a tablet to practice multiplication may help a child memorize facts for a test, but it does nothing to ignite her drive to devise an invention the world has never before seen.

The destructive confluence of decimated school budgets, neurotically locked-down technology, and lockstep assessment mandates is taking a toll on progressive educators—and disempowering students.

Our students deserve better. I believe one of the solutions to transforming education is the open source model.

The free and open source software movement is a philosophy and a practice born from the work of 20th-century hackers and programmers. It's much more than clever code and free software. Open source communities embrace principles of collaboration, participation, freedom, and trust. To work openly means to work cooperatively, to generously share knowledge, and to create a democratized culture where a diversity of contributions is encouraged and valued.

Consider Mozilla, the software community behind the Firefox web browser. Their mission illustrates the spirit of open:

> *Our mission is to ensure the Internet is a global public resource, open and accessible to all. An Internet that truly puts people first, where individuals can shape their own experience and are empowered, safe and independent. At Mozilla, we're a global community of technologists, thinkers and builders working together to keep the Internet alive and*

accessible, so people worldwide can be informed contributors and creators of the Web. We believe this act of human collaboration across an open platform is essential to individual growth and our collective future."

Like Mozilla, public schools aspire to cultivate shared learning communities where every student has opportunities for intellectual growth. But do open source principles work in the classroom? Can schools build successful technology programs on open source software? When students are engaged co-creators and trusted apprentices, does a new school community emerge?

The purpose of this book is to answer these questions. The stories draw from my 17 years serving as the Technology Director for Penn Manor School District, a public school system in Lancaster County, Pennsylvania. Open source software has been the heart of Penn Manor technology since 1999. Free and open source software helped our team build affordable and robust educational technology infrastructure. We've saved huge sums of district taxpayer money by trading expensive proprietary programs for open source counterparts.

However, the budget is only part of the story. Over time, the open source model reshaped our students' classroom experiences. The application of open source principles led to the development of a unique one-to-one learning program, in which we supplied thousands of middle and high school students with an unlocked district laptop running free and open source software exclusively. Our efforts culminated with an internationally recognized high school student help desk program built on a foundation of collaboration, community, participation, and trust. We found that open classrooms look more like art studios and makerspaces, and nothing like factories.

If you are a teacher, school administrator, technology director, or school board director seeking affordable and creative technology ideas, this book is for you. You don't need a degree in computer science to understand the concepts. I begin the first chapter with a lesson on open source software, reveal problems created by closed source software, and explain how the open source model offers solutions. We'll briefly review the history of software freedom and touch on the virtues of hacking. In chapter two, I share how open source software like Moodle and WordPress saved our district several hundred thousand dollars. And I'll explain how a few key learning projects became the foundation for our current student technology initiatives.

In chapter three, you'll meet Penn Manor's technology team and take a behind-the-scenes tour of our open source communication systems and infrastructure. We move out of the server room and into the elementary classroom in chapter four, Linux is Elementary. The switch from Mac to Linux laptops was an inflection point for our schools. I'll explain our urgency for cost savings, a rationale for the transition, and how we made it successful for elementary students and teachers.

The second half of the book documents how Penn Manor used the open source model to build a one-to-one technology learning program and unique student technology help desk. Even if your school decides not to go all-in with open source software, the Penn Manor story is loaded with cost-cutting tips, discussion points, and planning ideas that apply to most one-to-one device programs. Chapter five is a detailed account of the strategic planning that led to Penn Manor's one-to-one initiative. I'll discuss the district's guiding principles, educational objects, and rationale for providing students administrator rights to laptops they can fully control.

In chapter six, you'll meet Penn Manor's first student technology apprentices and read stories of their remarkable software creations and achievements. Chapter seven covers the one-to-one laptop pilot activities that helped us prepare for the start of the full program. I'll discuss teacher professional development workshops and recount a few unexpected snags we encountered during the pilot. Penn Manor's laptop software development practices conclude the chapter.

The one-to-one program takes flight in chapter eight. A concentrated three-week sprint unleashed 1,725 unlocked laptops into Penn Manor High School. When Penn Manor's open technology project ended, our students' new world of learning began. Student and teacher success stories steal the show in chapter nine, The Open Schoolhouse.

With more than 4000 student computers, Penn Manor School District maintains the largest public school fleet of free and open source laptops in Pennsylvania. It's a small start. We must liberate more students and classrooms. I offer our stories and my personal narrative as one model for schools to consider. I hope it starts a conversation because, as educators, our collective mission is to create exceptional student learning experiences. We can talk about apps, curriculum, devices, and test scores, but I think the most fundamental question is simple: On which side of the command line do our students stand?

Do we preset the classroom controls, lock-down learning, and prewire schools to run inside a closed technology sandbox?

Or do we embrace open, and empower students to change the world?

1
A Brief Open Source Lesson

Code is the heart of modern gadgets. Without a programmer's carefully planned playbook of instructions, our computers, phones, cars, and pacemakers are nothing more than inert rectangles of plastic, metal, and glass. It's nearly impossible to purchase an electronic device that isn't controlled by software. Marc Andreessen, technology entrepreneur and co-founder of Netscape, offers a lucid observation, "Software is eating the world."[1] With so much power concentrated in code, we ought to understand how software is made, controlled, and distributed. Let's discuss closed source software before we turn our attention to open source software concepts and principles.

Writing software is similar to movie production. To create the "Star Wars" films, Lucas and his team generated outlines, drafted and revised scripts, built sets, and filmed scenes. Next, editors and directors brought together footage and sound, cut errors, and sequenced the narrative to create a finished movie. The film was then packaged into a DVD or digital file for us to watch on the big screen or our little home laptop screen.

Software programs and apps are like a finished movie. A programmer's source code—the complete sequence of instructions, scripts, and commands required to make the software do your bidding—is compiled into a playable file which springs to life when you click or tap it. Like a movie on DVD, the completed software package is all we ever see. The cryptic bits of source code are boxed up inside the program.

Software can be classified as either closed source or open source. Adobe Photoshop is closed source; we receive the playable program only. The underlying computer code to rotate your family vacation photos, or touch up bad lighting on your cat's first birthday, is never visible to us. Adobe keeps Photoshop's source code under lock and key.

Many closed source, proprietary commercial programs are familiar household names: Microsoft Windows and Office, Apple's iOS and the MacOS operating system, Adobe's Creative Suite products, and business software like QuickBooks are common examples. In each case, the company holds the copyright and the code. Consumers can't examine, study, or copy the programming inside Windows or Photoshop. Like Lucas' unedited film footage, Windows and Photoshop source code is hidden from public view.

As you might expect, closed source software licensing protects business interests. When we purchase Photoshop, we receive a 'right to use' software license. We don't get the code and we can't alter the software. Without source code blueprints, and the permission to study or improve the software, we become renters of commercial programming property and must live by the landlord's rules.

Closed source software is often tightly ingrained in a device's identity. Apple's iPhone and iPad behave the way they do thanks to the company's closed source iOS operating system. Apple iOS is the software brain behind the phone's behaviors and buttons. Consumers do not directly pay for iOS software, yet it is indivisible from Apple devices. You can't buy an iPad or iPhone without iOS. And without iOS, an iPhone would be as useful as a tin-can phone. Furthermore, Apple prohibits—and actively discourages—customers from installing any other operating system on their iPhone or iPad. The software is closed, the hardware is closed, and Apple's trade secrets stay inside their corporate black box.

Closed Source Software

Closed source, proprietary software licenses grant several commercial powers. The first is pricing power. Let's say you recently launched a new lemonade stand and need special accounting software to run your business. If I am selling lemonade stand software, you might buy it. And if I am the only shop selling that kind of software, I can charge whatever you are willing to pay for a software license. You'll probably want to keep the software current, so I'll charge you for future version upgrades as well. And since you are a licensee of the software—and can't rewire the software yourself—you are at my mercy.

Dependency is the second power of closed source commercial software. Perhaps you unearth an amazing secret ingredient for a perfect lemonade mix. Congratulations! Your stand grows and sales boom.

A BRIEF OPEN SOURCE LESSON

Meanwhile, you have come to rely on my software and continuously add critical sales data into the system. Other lemonade accounting software programs may have appeared on the market, but eventually you reach a tipping point where the cost—and practicality—of switching to different software becomes unbearable. You have created lemonade so irresistible that your customers can't say "no," and I have created lemonade software so essential to your business that you can't walk away. Just as you have the secret recipe for sublime lemonade, I have my secret software code locked away from your control.

Software dependency is common in schools. When commercial programs like Microsoft Office, as well as proprietary document file formats, become entrenched and institutionalized into school curriculum, converting to alternatives becomes progressively more difficult and often unpopular.

The third power of closed source software is control. On a basic level, control means customers and educators are beholden to a world created by programmers. If I wrote your lemonade inventory software, you have no control over the sequence of buttons or screens that you use to produce your lemon supply report. My programming decisions define how you use my software. You may want, or need, additional reports and features, but I hold the classified code. Your wishes are granted by my programming wand and good will alone. You are now at the mercy of my software design. Good thing my intentions are pure, and I'm not a diabolical programmer, right?

But what if I were Evil Charlie, the dastardly lemonade software tyrant? If you can't read or review my code, how do you know what my program is doing below the surface of your screen? Could you detect that I've implanted a little spying bot that quietly watches your supply ordering activity and covertly grabs the ingredients for your secret lemonade recipe? Would you discover the hidden log tracking your sugar orders? I bet your sales information would be of great interest to your sugar vendors—or your competitors. Lucky for your lemonade empire, I'm not feeling evil. At least not at the moment.

Software Subscription Squeeze

Let's move on from the lemonade example and consider a commercial software purchasing model with a sour twist: pay-for-use software subscriptions. Think of a software subscription like a subscription to the New York Times. As long as we pay the monthly bill, we receive the latest paper on our doorstep.

With a traditional New York Times service subscription, we can archive previous issues as long as we would like—or as long as we have enough space in our basement. In contrast, software service subscriptions compel customers to immediately stop using the product if the subscription lapses. If we stop sending checks, the newspaper stops showing up at our doorstep.

Commercial software subscriptions create bitter problems for school budgets. One example is Adobe Creative Cloud—the software bundle that includes Photoshop, InDesign, and other creative program. Prior to 2014, schools could make a one-time purchase of a perpetual Photoshop license, and use the "boxed" version as long as it ran on school computers. Since Photoshop updates typically do not include features essential to classrooms, schools saved money by skipping versions and upgrading only when absolutely necessary, or when budgets allowed. Over the course of a decade, Penn Manor School District saved tens of thousands of dollars by skipping every other, or every third, paid Photoshop version upgrade.

In 2014, Adobe transitioned customers to the Creative Cloud software subscription rental model. Schools using Photoshop, InDesign and other Adobe products suddenly faced subscription fees in perpetuity. If a school stopped paying the regular fee, Adobe switched off the digital lights and rendered the software inactive.

To persuade schools to adopt the Creative Cloud rental service, Adobe stopped selling perpetual licenses with educational discounts. Without another program capable of accurately opening a Photoshop file, schools choosing to stick with Adobe became beholden to substantial subscription bills, forever. Imagine if your archived New York Times issues suddenly disappeared when you canceled your subscription service!

Microsoft is moving to a similar licensing model. The company's Enrollment for Education Solutions program is a rental arrangement whereby schools pay a yearly software subscription fee for the use of Office, Windows, and other Microsoft products. Pricing is determined by the total student and staff population count—larger schools pay more. As with Adobe's Creative Cloud, Microsoft's subscription license is not perpetual. If a school stops paying the subscription bill, it is required to immediately uninstall the software from every server and every student and teacher computer. The school is left with nothing.

A cloud-based learning management system (LMS) is another example of software tied to a subscription. Products such as Edmodo and Schoology do not allow schools to locally install the software on the servers a district owns. These LMS programs live inside vendor-controlled servers. The vendor locks up assignments, quizzes, videos, and classroom resource that teachers create in formats that the vendor, and only the vendor, controls. The cost and time commitment to migrate data out of these systems can be astronomical, if it is even possible to migrate at all.

Do you hear a certain '70s rock band singing in the distance? "You can check out anytime you like, but you can never leave." It's no surprise that technology companies prefer software subscriptions that generate consistent revenue, separate schools from source code, and tether students to systems under vendor control. The model is terrific for corporations, but is dreadful for district budgets and for educational freedom.

All children may be created equal, but school funding formulas are anything but fair. An affluent district may shrug off costs associated with commercial software subscriptions. But for schools that cannot afford to pay, yet another division is created between students who have access to software and those who do not.

There is also a deeper ethical problem: reliance on closed source proprietary software teaches students a lesson of dependence on secret technology they are powerless to examine, study, share, and improve upon. If the social mission of schools is to amplify student potential, disseminate knowledge, and prepare students to have an impact on the world, then schools have a duty to help kids be free thinkers and self-reliant architects of their futures.

As with most addictions, software dependency is largely psychological. Recovery requires an open mind, courage to change, and the will to make it happen.

What is Open Source Software?

The open source software movement is the creation of those who dreamed of freedom from commercial software limitations. Programmers renounced proprietary software agreements and licensed their code so anyone could use, read, modify, copy, study and share it. In the past two decades, millions of software developers and organizations have embraced the open source philosophy. Advocates believe collaboration, community, and sharing creates better software. The result is a colossal software trove offered for free, but with a pay-it-forward expectation that others will improve upon the code.

Today, open source software is everywhere. It quietly powers the Internet, our Android phones, televisions, and vehicles. Every time we search Google, our queries consult a mammoth server farm running on open source software. Open source software is found in our most mission-critical infrastructure and financial systems. Did you know trades on the New York Stock Exchange are powered by open source software? Your school computers may also be using open source software right now. The Firefox web browser and Moodle Learning Management System (LMS) are both common and widely adopted open source programs.

Open source software is frequently zero cost, but price is only half the story. It embodies an expression of liberty, and the ethical principle of sharing to drive innovation and learning. Free and open source licensing encourages us to read, modify, copy, and learn from the source code. The model shifts software control from corporations to a community where anyone is free to participate and contribute.

If we look past software programming, we discover the spirit in the open machine. Open source is a philosophy where principles of sharing one's work, meritocracy, transparency, and collaboration are deeply valued. Programmers involved in open source projects typically adhere to these guiding principles when writing new code and applications.

Open source communities tend to reject strict hierarchies. Decision making is distributed and often decentralized. Everyone is free to participate, and merit is based on one's abilities and contributions, not one's social or organizational rank.

I think the Stone Soup fable eloquently ties together the ethos of open source. It is an old European folktale with many variations, but it typically goes something like this: An unfamiliar traveler arrives in a village and begins asking the townsfolk for help and food. The townsfolk are at first guarded and unwilling to share anything with this random stranger. After his requests for assistance go unanswered, the traveler tries a different strategy. He pulls out a large cooking pot, starts a fire, adds water, drops a few stones into the cooking pot, and starts stirring the concoction.

Curiosity overwhelms the villagers. They approach and ask what he is brewing. The stranger replies that he is making Stone Soup. It will be wonderful, but it is a work in progress and needs a little extra something to improve the flavor. Could they help contribute to the soup? One-by-one, others inquire about the soup, offer to help, and begin adding ingredients and seasoning. More villagers bring bread, meats, and other treats. Over the course of the evening, the traveler and the townsfolk work together to prepare a feast shared with the entire village.

What is the moral of the Stone Soup tale? On one level, we might identify the stranger as an archetypal trickster who manipulates an entire town into preparing a free meal using little more than roadside gravel!

However, there is a more profound meaning: Cooperation, collaboration and trust can benefit an entire village. The traveler didn't grab the meal and run. He shared the feast with the village folk. He modeled a better way to work together and took the initiative to get it started.

When we rally around a common goal and share our work with others, we create something new, something that we can be proud of sharing, something that can change and transform our world. This is the spirit of the open source community.

Software Communities of Practice

Remember that lemonade stand? Let's say I decide to write a little program to track lemon inventory for my juice stand. I could keep it to myself and toil away on new features alone. My efforts will move as quickly as I can work, which could mean progress is as slow as dial-up. And my program's usefulness will be limited to my imagination and programming abilities. It might not amount to much.

What if I make the source code publicly available for others to review and modify, for free? Could it grow? Some might take the program and run—probably without bothering to send a thank-you card. Others might provide feedback in the form of feature requests, complaints, or pleas for support. But those with a passion for lemonade software will do something powerful—they will study the code, add to it, and share their contributions. Lemonade aficionados will create new reports, add attractive yellow icons, fix bugs, and perhaps even perform a security review. As programmers contribute layer after layer of new functionality, the effect of their community contributions is a new software tool that a solo programmer couldn't create alone.

Virtual communities of practice are central to the creation and evolution of open source software. Shared passion brings like-minded individuals together to create and improve software across a massive range of interests. Small software projects may be reared by a couple of dedicated individuals. Large, complex projects may have thousands of contributors. The work is typically transparent and often inclusive; those who wish to participate need not necessarily be celebrity programmers. Involvement can range from answering questions in an online forum and writing documentation to submitting bug reports and beta testing new features. Diversity of talents is key; each new code contribution, bug report, tutorial, and training video helps a project grow.

The accretion of individual contributions, the additive effect of cooperation, and a community growth mindset makes open source compelling for educators. As we will discover, the open source community model shares considerable similarities with a vibrant learning community. It takes a village to raise a child; it also takes a community to cultivate and grow great software. It turns out that hackers are outstanding members of the open source community.

Hacking and Software Freedom

Open source software is sometimes misunderstood as a weird playground for mad degenerate hackers who spend dark nights scheming up nefarious plots for social, political, and moral disruption. Popular media commonly associates hacking with the wanton destruction of financial systems, credit card theft, and cybercrime. High school principals may fear a modern Ferris Bueller infiltrating a school computer system and changing attendance records.

The original hacker subculture had nothing to do with crime. At MIT in the 1960s, hacking represented a playful, artistic, and wily approach to pushing the boundaries of electronics and software. Computer science students found joy in the intellectual challenge of overcoming a program's limitations, or extending technology to do something new. Software and hardware hacks were valued for technical dexterity and creativity. Pioneering activist and hacker Judith Milhon—better known by her online handle 'St. Jude'—described hacking as "the clever circumvention of imposed limits, whether imposed by your government, your IP server, your own personality, or the laws of physics."[2] If you have ever repaired a leaking water faucet using masking tape, bird feathers and silly string—at 2 a.m. on a Sunday morning—you have felt the rapture of home improvement hacking.

Roots of the free and open source software movement can be traced to the MIT hacker community. Richard Stallman, a programmer with the MIT Artificial Intelligent Lab during the 1980s, was frustrated by the inability to access and study the source code of a proprietary Xerox lab printer. Without the source code, or the legal authorization to request it, he was unable to explore, extend or otherwise hack the printer to be more useful for the MIT community.

Commercial software limitations stirred Stallman to action. He began work on a new computer operating system called, GNU.[3] Stallman pushed further and did something unheard of in the early 1980s: he gave the entire software system away, at no cost, and with an assurance that it will always be free. He outlined his reasoning in a paper titled The GNU Manifesto.

Stallman wrote: "I consider that the Golden Rule requires that if I like a program I must share it with other people who like it. Software sellers want to divide the users and conquer them, making each user agree not to share with others. I refuse to break solidarity with other users in this way. I cannot in good conscience sign a nondisclosure agreement or a software license agreement. So that I can continue to use computers without dishonor, I have decided to put together a sufficient body of free software so that I will be able to get along without any software that is not free."[4]

In 1989, Stallman crystallized his vision into the GNU Public License (GPL). The GPL upended restrictive commercial software licenses and introduced liberties and rights Stallman believed every citizen should have. Last revised in 1991, the GPL Free Software Definition[5] outlines four software freedoms:

Freedom 0. You have the freedom to run the program, for any purpose.

Freedom 1. You have access to the source code, the freedom to study how the program works, and the freedom to change it to make it do what you wish.

Freedom 2. You have the freedom to redistribute copies of the original program so you can help your neighbor.

Freedom 3. You have the freedom to distribute copies of your modified versions to others. By doing this you can give the whole community a chance to benefit from your changes.

The GNU project attracted others who believed in the mission and possessed the technical expertise to chip in and build upon Stallman's work. GNU flourished and expanded to include a broad set of fundamental tools for software development—many of which are still widely used today. Momentum for the GNU system grew, but a playful student lit the fuse and launched free and open source operating systems into the future.

Linux: From Finland with Love

August 1991 was a time of software revolution. Sir Tim Berners-Lee published the first World Wide Web page on August 6, 1991.[6] Against the backdrop of tremendous geopolitical transformation in Eastern Europe, a young Finnish computer science student named Linus Torvalds was about to spark another revolution. While a student at the University of Helsinki, Torvalds began writing a new operating system. Little did he know, his learning exercise would alter the course of computing.

On August 25, 1991, Torvalds posted an Internet message on the Minux Internet Usenet newsgroup[7] and gave birth to the project later dubbed Linux: "I'm doing a (free) operating system (just a hobby, won't be big and professional like gnu) for 386(486) AT clones."[8] Torvalds adopted an open and collaborative approach from the start. He shared his new operating system and accepted feedback and contributions from enthusiasts who wished to help improve his work. As the project attracted developers, Torvalds licensed Linux under the terms of Stallman's GPL, thus ensuring it would remain free to use, study, and improve upon in perpetuity.

A dedicated volunteer community rallied behind Linux. Driven by enthusiasm, programmers contributed new features into the fledgling operating system. In the time between the initial launch in 1991 and 2001, Linux accumulated thousands of new contributors. By the time it reached version 2.4, Linux had swelled to over three million lines of code.

Linux was the missing link in Stallman's GNU software project. Communities of hackers merged the components of GNU with the new Linux code. The result was the first truly free and open operating system: GNU/Linux—which we now simply call Linux.

Today, Linux embodies what is possible when a community embraces and acts on free software and open source principles. Linux has grown to more than 21 million lines of code.[9] More than 12,000 world-wide programmers have contributed to the project. Individuals, as well as corporations such as Google, Red Hat, and Samsung, continuously create, bug-test and submit hundreds of Linux updates—called patches—every day.[10] It is a global software project in perpetual motion.

Linux is the software foundation for a staggering number of modern technologies. You'll find Linux inside devices like Android phones, smart televisions, cars, Raspberry PIs, and the wireless router in your home. The Internet runs on Linux—it is the control center inside the webservers and routers that connect us to friends, family, and cats across the world. Amazon, Google, IBM, NASA, The New York Stock Exchange, and the world's top 500 world supercomputers all run Linux—not bad for a free student hobby project.

The GPL and Linux creation stories are meaningful because they provide context and background on the genesis of free and open source software. The actions of Stallman and Torvalds demonstrate commitment to an ethos of sharing, collaboration, and the freedom to learn. Both pioneers valued community and colleagues. Both instigated a movement born from passion. I suspect they had no way of knowing just how far their waves would travel and that, decades later, their work would help schools like Penn Manor ignite a new culture of educational hacking, sharing, and student empowerment.

2
Beginnings and Foundations

Penn Manor School District's transformation into an open schoolhouse begins with primordial creation stories. Unlike Athena, our technology systems did not spring fully formed from the minds of the IT staff or school principals. However, a few epic headaches heralded the birth of new technology initiatives.

In the late 1990's the district had experimented with a few free and open source software programs. Staff email ran on qmail, a public domain email program. The district website ran on the open source Apache software program. These programs lived cheerfully on a server running a flavor of Linux produced by Red Hat, a company based in North Carolina. Red Hat Linux is one of many varieties of Linux called "distributions." Since the late 1990s, Red Hat has been selling a pre-packaged, pre-assembled, Linux mix that people could quickly install—although, "quick" is a relative term. At the time, servers ran on blazingly slow Intel Pentium III processors, and Red Hat Linux was installed from a CD shipped in a cardboard box (yes, software-in-a-box was once real).

Free and open source software adoption at Penn Manor was driven, in large part, by the word free. Technology that cost nothing was attractive, especially to members of our public who were unconvinced that the Internet—and school technology in general—was anything more than a fad. And some predicted computing might be on the verge of collapse once the much feared Y2K software bug threw society into a technology stone-age.

In October 1999, I became the Technology Director after a year of working as a school building technician. My immediate priority was riding out a possible Y2K crisis. The computer apocalypse scare ended with a whimper, but my next task was far more world-changing: developing a new grade book program for teachers.

A New Grade Book

Our grading software needed a serious update. Before the turn of the century, teachers wrestled with a combination of Excel spreadsheets, paper, and a rickety grade book program from a commercial vendor. We needed an easy-to-use, paperless, web-based grade book, and parent grade report web portal. Today, online student progress systems are common. But at the time, posting student grade and attendance records online was a scary proposition.

Commercial software solutions left me with two nagging concerns. Cost was, of course, a problem. Traditional software companies, with traditional proprietary development toolkits, certainly knew how to generate traditionally large bills. A community bake sale wasn't going to cut it.

My second concern was more troubling. If we selected closed source software, my team would have no access to the underlying code and no ability to customize the program to suit the needs of our teachers. Our faculty had great ideas for an online grade book. After all, they would be using the software every day, and they knew exactly what they wanted. But vendors didn't guarantee our requested features would be included.

Why would we exclude our staff from participating in the design and development of their key applications? I contemplated a better option—but it was risky.

I chose to partner with a talented software developer named James Ming. Far from a nefarious hacker with a shady back story, James was a talented and professional programmer. James and his team collaborated with Penn Manor teachers, administrators, technology staff, and parents to build the grade book we needed. He deftly translated teacher needs into programming lingo and incorporated requests like assignment quick-fills, sorting, and reporting. Working together, we added icon designs and visual elements from staff feedback.

At times, it felt like a Silicon Valley technology startup, minus the pinball machines, gourmet food, and onsite massages. After a few short but energetic months, we had designed, developed, and deployed a locally hosted web grade book, customized by teacher input, principal requirements, and parent requests.

The result was extraordinary—we had the grade book teachers needed, had access to the code, and saved a bundle of money. Our program launched in December 2001, and Penn Manor School District became the first public school district in Pennsylvania to offer real-time parent access to live grade and attendance information for every middle and high school student.

James called the system Lettergrade. In 2001, it was a huge leap forward for parent communication. Before Lettergrade, progress reports and report cards were mailed home eight times a year. The information was outdated by the time it landed in a parent's mailbox. The web system turned the decades-old reporting timeline upside down. Parents could now track their child's assignments, grades, and attendance in near real-time via a secure web portal. Open access to their child's grades provided a starting point for parents to discuss what happened in school that day, and fostered better communication between parents and teachers.

At the time, I estimated the total cost savings for the Lettergrade solution to be approximately $100,000, compared with a commercial grade book system. Working collaboratively with James and his team, the district dodged a hefty software bill. The savings were the direct result of a creative partnership, tenacious teachers willing to take a risk, and open source software.

LAMP Lights Learning

The Lettergrade software license was not open source, but the system was created using an open source bundle called LAMP. It might sound like a fancy lighting fixture for tech hipsters, but LAMP is an acronym for a quartet of tightly integrated open source software tools for building web sites. The four ingredients are: Linux, the server operating system; Apache, software to deliver web pages to your browser; MySQL, a database; and PHP, computer code to make web pages act like desktop programs.

Push aside the curtain on your favorite websites, and you'll likely find a variation of the great and powerful LAMP humming away. The software quartet is popular among the web crowd for multiple technical reasons—and it is entirely free to use. That means developers can build quality websites without taking out a second mortgage or selling a kidney.

Free software like LAMP keep costs down, but the Lettergrade developers also could connect with a community of fellow programmers from whom they could draw ideas and coding tricks. Over time, the Lettergrade system grew beyond a basic gradebook and web portal. As our software development relationship matured, my staff helped

Lettergrade expand to include online student course registration tools, a curriculum database, and elementary school report cards.

An open source LAMP core provided one more advantage: control. With the whole system open to us, my team and I could review the code at any point. We could simply walk up to the server, switch on a monitor, and dive into the workings of the program, or review our student data. My team could also easily audit security. Free from vendor controls, we had a data migration escape plan. Should we need to move on to another system, student data was easy to extract from Lettergrade. These advantages imprinted open source values on the Penn Manor Technology Team. Those values are still part of our decision-making today.

Frozen Server, Flowing Tears

Lettergrade was great, but not perfect. Neither was my judgment. As the project progressed, I learned a hard leadership lesson. During the project's second year, we planned to launch online elementary report cards. At the end of the first marking period, hundreds of elementary teachers would transfer final student subject grades and progress comments from paper and spreadsheets to the new online grading portal. It was to be the grand debut of our glorious elementary report card system. The data entry day was scheduled for Friday, October 31, 2003. Little did I know the day would be a horror show.

Human error triggered a monstrous server crash the night before our system debut on Halloween. Around 9 p.m., our new report card system was spewing a terrible cacophony of random characters on otherwise blank web pages. The Lettergrade programmers, district system engineer Shawn Beard, and I jumped into action. Student data was safe and secure, but the server itself was scrambled like a smashed pumpkin. It needed a complete software rebuild. Fast.

After a lengthy night of brisk work, the server was restored and ready for the big launch. I plodded home around 5 a.m. and promptly collapsed into bed. The first emergency calls started 60 minutes later.

Early rising teachers had hit a wall. They expected to beat the data entry rush before colleagues arrived, but our new report card website was grinding to a near halt. Web pages wouldn't load, nothing was saving. The system shambled like a mummy. Some struggled for over an hour to enter just a few report card grades. Tears were flowing and tempers flared—the usually polite elementary teachers had a few ghastly words about the new system that morning.

As the programmers worked on the problem, I traveled from school to school and apologized to the rightfully frustrated teachers. I felt absolutely awful about the mess, but I owed staff a personal visit to openly talk about the server problems. Fortunately, the technical trouble was resolved by mid-afternoon and the day ended on a somewhat positive note.

So what happened? Did open source software fail us? Not at all. The server hardware was the culprit. The server lacked the processing muscle to handle hundreds of simultaneous data transactions. Like the "all circuits are busy" message from the old telephone systems, the district server dropped web connections as it became overloaded. As more teachers logged on, the situation became worse, and the entire system slowed to a crawl.

The system crunch happened long before modern server tricks and fast hardware. Today, when servers are super busy, a system administrator can wave her hands over the keyboard and quickly create additional capacity. We were working from one sad little beige box. And that was my mistake. I should have planned better and not put all of our digital goodies in one technology bag.

But I learned a valuable lesson that day: when you fail, own the mistake and be open and honest with your community. They deserve the truth and will respect you for being candid.

Apart from the dramatic server meltdown, the Lettergrade project was a success, and Penn Manor School District relied on the system for several years. The need for a modern student management system ultimately drove us to another vendor. But the original Lettergrade beta design experience demonstrated the power of engaging teachers in collaborative technology projects. District staff rallied together as a do-it-yourself community of software makers. If the practice worked for teachers and the technology team, what would happen if students came together to create their own classroom computers?

A Better School Assembly Line

Shawn Beard and I had a crazy idea in the spring of 2001. How much money could we save if we built our own white-box desktop computers? No neighboring school district had tried it, probably because the effort to assemble a hundred computers from scratch would be tremendous. Yet, the cost savings were attractive, and we wanted to define exactly what components were included in district computers.

Shawn's inventive, do-it-yourself attitude was evident the first time I interviewed him. His hobby list is a mashup between extreme outdoor adventures and home improvement challenges. He's the person you want on your team when the zombie apocalypse comes to town and puts the IT crowd on the unemployment line. Shawn's thirst for a challenge has always been strong. That spring, he was brave enough to trust students with our in-house computer build plan.

For a three-year period between the summer of 2001 and 2003, Shawn and the technology team worked with several student apprentices to assemble new PC desktops entirely in-house. At the time, it was considered a radical computer procurement practice (schools typically purchased preassembled desktop computers). We saved more than $120,000 by buying large quantities of individual PC components and building 600 systems ourselves. However, the new opportunity for collaborative student learning was more exciting than the cost-savings.

More than two dozen students in middle and high school took part in the PC assembly program. All students with an interest in computers were encouraged to help, but most of the young builders had recently completed a Cisco Networking Academy course at Penn Manor High School. Many of the students planned to pursue technical careers after graduation.

The build events were multi-day summer festivals. We commandeered large classrooms and setup a multi-station assembly line. At the first station, students would unbox and inventory parts. At the next station, students would snap processors and RAM into logic boards. Students at the third and fourth stations would prep cases and wire together components. The last station was for final testing and QA. Students would intermittently switch jobs, which ensured that everyone had a chance to learn each step of the computer assembly process.

At first, Shawn and I were apprehensive—our knuckles were as white as the PC cases. What if the eager student apprentices destroyed a carton full of processors or damaged fragile RAM chips? What if they miswired the logic board power cables and cooked the whole works? The resulting pyrotechnics might be momentarily dazzling, but lots of money could burn in a flash. But no fire alarms tripped—and the kids loved it. They were cautious with the delicate components. Accidental damage rates during the build were as low as we would expect from the adults. I could have counted the number of ruined components on two hands—and that includes the one CPU on which I inadvertently bent the pins!

The student apprentices loved working side-by-side with staff on a project with clear and tangible results. They were personally building classroom computers for fellow students. As the young builders signed their names to the inside of the PC cases, a sense of ownership and pride was evident. Educators talk about engaging students with authentic learning experiences—a student assembling the very computer used in her classes has to be near the top of the engagement scale.

My team held three summer computer build festivals, and each event attracted students who typically did not participate in traditional extracurricular school activities. Often, students who are technically gifted, but socially reserved, have trouble finding activities that both motivate and challenge. Students on the build team became involved in a school activity outside of the classroom, and the opportunity helped instill a sense of confidence and belonging to a community of learners.

Parents and senior citizen volunteers donated time to the construction process as well. Shelby Foster, our new school building systems technician, even enlisted her dad to help manually sort screws. Community members expressed overwhelming support. Taxpayers were pleased the district found novel ways to cut costs while providing real-world technology learning opportunities.

Penn Manor School District received the 2004 Pennsylvania School Business Officials Award of Achievement as a result of the PC build program.[11] Eventually, classroom laptops replaced desktops, and the cost of preassembled PCs dropped to the point where it was less cost effective to build custom systems. But the seeds of our current one-to-one Student Help Desk program were planted during those summer computer build festivals, and another brick was added to our open schoolhouse.

Moodle Learning Management System

Long before Facebook, Twitter, and WordPress made web publishing easy, building a classroom website was an epic adventure. Teachers attending Penn Manor's summer 2002 web design workshops dived into HTML coding and Adobe Dreamweaver software. Six hours later, they surfaced with a basic classroom webpage. And given limited time for professional development, basic it would stay. No wonder—changes were no labor of love. To update their sites, teachers would open HTML files in Dreamweaver, struggle with the code, and send the revised pages to the IT team, which would upload the file to the district webserver. If something was askew, or if we noticed a typo, the process started all over again. It was a royal pain for busy educators.

Teachers needed better software to create classroom webpages and online learning communities. I began scouting for an affordable system that was easy to use, flexible, learner-centric, and open. Commercial web publishing systems and learning management system (LMS) packages crowded the marketplace. Blackboard and WebCT—two of the most popular proprietary systems—were endorsed by our regional Intermediate Unit (an educational services agency for Lancaster County). Neighboring school districts signed on with Blackboard, which created some peer pressure for Penn Manor to do the same. However, Blackboard carried a price tag of more than $50,000. Plus, we would have no ability to change, enhance, or modify the software code. It was like the proprietary grade book situation all over again.

I discovered the solution on Monday, November 11, 2002, at 9:49 p.m. That night, I created an account on the Moodle.org community forum.[12]

Today, Moodle is the leading free and open source LMS. It is installed in 230 countries and has more than 70 million users worldwide.[13] But in 2002, Moodle was an unknown player in a space dominated by commercial giants. Moodle was unique, however. Schools were free to download and run the program on local servers at no cost, and educators were encouraged to modify the code to serve their needs. Moodle's open attitude didn't end with licensing. The inventor, Martin Dougiamas, wrote software to support learning in the context of community, collaboration, and constructionism. Dougiamas valued software freedom and learner freedom. He was a teacher and a programmer.

Shawn installed Moodle on our internal servers in late 2002. After a few months of private testing with my team, I conducted the first Moodle workshops with a small group of teachers in June 2003. Early adopters loved it. No crash course in cryptic HTML, CSS, or FTP commands was needed. Teachers were comfortable with Moodle in under three hours.

The following summer, our Moodle workshops expanded to 150 Penn Manor teachers, and classroom use soared. Moodle wasn't a forced teaching requirement, but faculty and staff adopted the program with exuberance. Moodle was used by nearly 50 percent of district teachers by December 2004. Before Moodle, only 10 percent of district staff created a web page. Adoption skyrocketed because Moodle took the complexity out of creating web pages. It let teachers focus on publishing content.

Quiz tools were popular. Math and Language Arts teachers used Moodle to create practice exams for the Pennsylvania System of School Assessment (PSSA) tests, something that would have been impossible for them to develop in HTML. Moodle was also the catalyst for a makeover of a traditional Family and Consumer Class (FCS) classroom. Students at our two middle school buildings used Moodle to collaborate on a team research project. Students who never met face-to-face worked entirely online and discovered how to communicate and work on a virtual team. Today, this is commonplace. But in 2004, few schools had students working remotely from multiple locations.

Penn Manor School District's former Assistant Superintendent, Ellen Pollock, often said: "There can never be too much school-to-home communication." Ellen recognized the potential of technology to open lines of dialogue between parents, students, and teachers. Moodle gave parents a chance to look inside the content of classes and to be active agents in their child's education. Parents were especially pleased to have direct access to lesson content, classroom materials, and discussion forums.

Today Moodle continues to be our district LMS even as a new generation of closed source programs compete for school customers. Commercial system, such as Edmodo and Schoology, are delivered exclusively via Software as a Service (SaaS) subscription. With a closed source LMS subscription, schools have no local install option and no choice of maintaining their own private systems. And pricing for subscription-based LMS systems can be steep. Using an estimated cost of $5 per student, Penn Manor would pay over $20,000 per year—indefinitely—for a subscription to a system like Schoology. Those stakes are high when you consider that the longer a school uses an LMS, the pain of moving troves of content increases dramatically. I sleep comfortably knowing that Moodle will always be free and open to our students and staff.

Moodle could be a closed-source proprietary business, but true to its mission, it remains a community-driven open source project. While attending the 2015 MoodleMoot US conference in Minneapolis, I could feel the intense passion emanating from the founder, core developers, and warm user community. And it is community love that differentiates successful open source projects from software created by corporations. The Moodle community gave our schools a fantastic learning system. It empowered our classrooms and enabled my team to make even bigger bets on open source software.

Open Campus, Open Schools

Moodle is the e-learning environment powering our virtual high school consortium project, Open Campus PA. Launched in December 2011, Open Campus PA is the online learning partnership between Penn Manor School District and two neighboring Lancaster county school districts, Hempfield and Manheim Township. Open Campus PA attempts to blur the boundaries of traditional high school buildings and district attendance areas. With an open enrollment policy, students from any of the three districts may enroll in online courses taught by teachers from each partner high school. Courses are then conducted online for integrated groups of students from all three high schools.

The goal of the Open Campus PA partnership is to provide quality education choices for students seeking flexible schedules and specific elective courses not offered at their high school. In practice, the high school concept transforms into a truly unbounded learning community and looks much less like a monolithic silo where instruction exclusively occurs on site.

Free and open source software and open curriculum resources are, of course, central to Open Campus PA. In fact, the Open Campus PA partnership resembles an open source software community in many ways. To maximize our ability to collaborate across districts, as well as reduce costs, all three participating districts create courses in a shared Moodle system. Teacher development teams work in person, and remotely, to cooperatively build Moodle courses across a range of subjects. A challenge, of course, is to wrangle content from three different high schools, which often leads to heated discussions, healthy debate, and a touch of friction. However, the best ideas usually win, and teachers quickly move forward with the real work of course development.

WordPress Classroom Publishing

I think of Moodle and WordPress as fraternal twins. Passionate and ingenious founders with ardent beliefs in free and open source software created both software platforms. Global communities of programmers, designers, and end users drive the development of both platforms. They use similar web technologies (LAMP), and subscribe to principles of simplicity and ease of use. They are credited with creating, and disrupting, entire industries. And they made dramatic impacts on our students, teachers, and staff.

WordPress is a content management and personal publishing platform that began life as a blogging engine. Released by co-founder Matt Mullenweg in 2003, WordPress' growth has been extraordinary. As of June 2016, it is found in the server rooms of approximately 26% of all websites.[14] WordPress is released under the terms of the GPL, which helps ensure the software will remain free and open in perpetuity.[15]

Penn Manor's first locally installed WordPress site, the PM Technology Blog, went live on July 5, 2007. It was conceived as the central hub for district technology communication and ruminations. It was also a proving ground for a much larger project: the transformation of school webpages from static HTML pages into attractive and easy-to-use web sites for parents and the public.

Since the late 1990's, Penn Manor's district and school websites were created and maintained by the IT Team. I'd be remiss to not mention that for the longest time, I loved building our websites from scratch. Web design was a part of my early technology career, and tinkering with the district site was something I enjoyed. However, the job of managing a growing district IT department left me with less time for website care and feeding. Plus, we were publishing much more content, and I needed to get out of the file upload business. It was time to shop for a publishing system that would make us more efficient. WordPress was that system.

I could have turned to a proprietary school website platform like Schoolwires to solve the publishing problem. That would have cost the district $18,000 to $20,000 annually. In addition to the massive bill, our content would be chained to the vendor, perhaps for decades. I could not, in good faith, trade our freedom for convenience.

In spring 2008, we launched blogs.pennmanor.net, the web publishing network we still use today. The IT Team and I installed WordPress MU, an early variation of WordPress designed for multiple distinct websites. Between the spring of 2008 and the summer of 2010, we converted all school building, department, and district webpages to self-hosted WordPress sites. No external contractors, developers or designers were involved in the project. The WordPress community gave us the tools to do it ourselves, and the results were terrific.

The new publishing network wasn't just for school or office content. Hundreds of teachers and staff requested a blog for everything from classroom communication to student council community sites and everything in-between. Classroom blog sites hosted student writing and became outlets for debate and discussion via the WordPress comment system. Even our superintendent began blogging. It was exhilarating to watch how quickly teachers and staff adopted the system—few district technology initiatives caught on as rapidly.

The beauty of WordPress is that it handles the hardest bits of website coding while simultaneously providing the end-user total control over the site appearance and content. Teachers love playing with their blog site theme, colors, and graphics. And WordPress is famously simple to use. Teachers and school administrative assistants don't fumble with complicated screens full of commands that look to be on loan from chemistry textbooks. Training takes less than 30 minutes, after which, teachers can post content and navigate the blog like a pro.

WordPress is incredibly extensible. If you need a particular solution for a specific feature on your school website, there's a good chance someone in the community has already written a code module, called a WordPress Plugin, to satisfy your need.[16] My team drew from a catalog of WordPress Plugin modules to add features we could not create ourselves. We also connected other open source tools to create a blog aggregator page (planet.pennmanor.net) which collects new blog posts into a centralized district news stream.

Penn Manor's WordPress sites have received millions of visits from parents, community members, and alumni. By 2010, we estimated that Penn Manor maintained the largest self-hosted K-12 school WordPress network in Pennsylvania. The PA School Public Relations Association honored Penn Manor's blogging and social media initiatives with a 2010 Communications Award of Honor.[17] WordPress was a great solution for the district, but the story got better when high school journalism students took over the Penn Manor High School newsroom.

Freedom of the Student Press

For decades, the Penn Manor High School student newspaper, Penn Points, probably looked much like the school newspaper of your youth. A group of student journalists wrote articles, took photos, and assembled the paper inside layout software like Quark or Adobe InDesign. The student team printed several hundred copies a few times a year, and the vast majority of the papers ended up in the recycle bin. A time-intensive composition and printing process produced a print publication delivered to a narrow audience inside the high school building itself. The process begged for a makeover. It just needed the right software and a teacher looking for a new project. WordPress was the software and in August of 2009, we had a teacher ready to take on the challenge.

Susan Baldrige, a former reporter for Lancaster Newspapers who taught English at Penn Manor High School, had just taken over as the journalism class teacher and club advisor. I first met Susan in 2001—she was the Lancaster Newspaper reporter who broke the story about the district's Lettergrade online grade book program. Susan and I spoke at length about taking the traditional Penn Points paper and moving it to a web-only publication. We recognized the path was uncharted. She was just as eager and open-minded as I remembered from the Lettergrade news interview. I knew we had the teacher who could make the online student newspaper happen.

Today, it's funny to think an online publication sparked controversy. Back in 2009, many U.S. high schools were still without dedicated building websites, let alone online student newspapers. We had support from high school and district administration, but some staff criticism of the idea was scathing. Colleagues denounced the idea as risky. What if kids published something inappropriate? A teacher who wished to retain the legacy in-house print program questioned why we would discontinue teaching traditional printing skills. Others remarked that we were a little bonkers for giving kids that much control over a public website. One disparaging comment made the hair on the back of my neck bristle: "Who would bother reading an online student newspaper?"

Susan and I decided from the beginning the revised Penn Points newspaper would be as open and inclusive as possible. As September commenced, we began soliciting student input during in-class design charrettes. The journalism students could weigh in on site colors, theme composition, graphics, artwork, and news column categories. Susan coordinated the discussions, and I began modifying a prebuilt WordPress theme that encompassed the class feedback and ideas.

We planned a fast debut for the new site. As I worked with several students to customize WordPress, other students began writing articles for the forthcoming news magazine. Student editors were selected and trained on WordPress management, and others were hurriedly working on artwork. Launch momentum was building, and the entire class was buzzing with excitement.

After four weeks of vigorous work, www.pennpoints.net debuted in October 2009. Titled "Penn Points – The Student News Magazine of Penn Manor High School," it was Pennsylvania's first online, nonprint high school newspaper. Penn Points received more than 6,000 visits in the first week. The student team was overjoyed.

A digital publication had immediate benefits. Environmental savings were huge—no longer would the school print thousands of paper pages each year. Susan noted: "No paper, no toner, printing." And the student writers were afforded publication speed. The concept of scheduled editions vaporized. Students published stories directly to the web as soon as the article was approved. Journalism students had the freedom to publish anytime—just like the professionals do.

Students could create work they cared about, to a real audience, who in turn interacted with the writers via article comments and feedback. Penn Points was suddenly more than a classroom assignment; it was a community news source. Sarah Schaeffer, a Penn Points Student Editor quipped: "It's really impressive for Penn Manor because no one really knows who we are, and 80,000 people all over the world can access it."[18]

With the web visitor count climbing, motivation to write and publish intensified. Students became keenly aware of which articles were generating the most views and used the data to guide future articles. Susan led story idea sessions and helped students pursue articles that pushed the boundaries of typical high school journalism. Controversial articles were popular. Stories on the dangers of chewing tobacco, teen pregnancy and sex, online privacy, and a local crime were provocative and artfully written. As student journalistic skills improved, the paper attracted even more readers. In the first year, Penn Points transformed from a traditional limited-run high school paper into a dynamic student news site with more than 100,000 visitors.

The National Scholastic Press Association recognized Penn Points with a 2010 Pacemaker Award, an extraordinary distinction for an online student publication in its first year of existence.[19] Awards aside, the most significant lesson of the Penn Points project is that a participatory open source classroom design can ignite student creativity and talent. Susan trusted her students and shaped nearly every element of the classroom experience to resemble a professional newsroom. She honored student agency and passion and reshaped a conventional journalism class into a cutting-edge collaborative community of practice driven by common goals. At first sight, an observer may have been alarmed by the classroom's seemingly messy, nearly chaotic structure. Upon closer inspection, one would see students immersed in the real journalistic work of interviewing, editing, pitching, and creating. It was authentic learning at its very finest.

Like the student computer build program, the Penn Points experience is another example of what happens when students are trusted to be full participants in learning. In both projects, learning power is transferred from the teacher to the student. By de-emphasizing the teacher as the fountain of all knowledge, students are empowered to ask better questions and inspired to create meaningful solutions. That's not to say a teacher is not necessary. Rather, her role is vital. She is the producer, her feedback and prompts guiding students along a cooperative, and open, learning journey.

Koha - A Library Gift

Sometimes it is much easier to go with what we know. We might buy the same coffee from the same local shop every day at the same time. We might order the same dish from a favorite restaurant, at every visit. We select a favorite car, dish soap, or chewing gum and cling to the brand with zealous ferocity. Educators often stick to practices and programs that are both traditional and familiar. It's not hard to understand why such groupthink is prevalent. If you were a school superintendent and every other school in your state was serving Hershey's chocolate bars in the cafeteria, would you dare to offer a generic alternative from Charlie's House of Confections? It can be tough to make choices that run counter to popular opinion. Fortunately, Penn Manor's library staff is a team of fearless open-minded adventurers.

In the spring of 2009, the library circulation system and catalog software ran Circ+, a Follett Corp. product that was rapidly approaching the end of its serviceable life. Follett is a major commercial player in school library software, textbooks, and school resource management. At the time, Follett encouraged customers to purchase its next-generation Integrated Library System (ILS), a product called Destiny Library Manager.

From a company like Follett, encouragement feels more like a forced march. Our Circ+ software was freezing up almost daily due to hard-coded database memory limits. Library staff were increasingly frustrated and longed for a solution, but Follett's support team was, unsurprisingly, not very helpful. My team couldn't provide much relief. The database was at the functional limit.

Follett's technical support staff didn't have a solution, but their sales reps certainly did; install Follett's new Destiny library software. The price to implement the new platform was about $50,000, with data conversion costing extra. As you might guess, we were appalled by the idea of repurchasing a system we already licensed. Unsolvable technical support issues, closed source software, and product discontinuations are useful implements of corporate lock-in. The company was unapologetic. So we decided that Destiny would not be our fate.

The library staff and my team began evaluating alternative library software systems. Never a group to mince words, Penn Manor's librarians and library assistants drew up a list of wants and demands, or "wamands", as they affectionately called them. They had a clear list of essential features and functions to handle cataloging, circulation, and searching. After a review of options, including a few commercial systems, the team selected Koha.

Koha is a free, community-driven library management system developed by teams of programmers and librarians worldwide. It's a full-featured, Integrated Library System (ILS) and the world's first fully open source ILS. Taking its name from the Maori custom of gift-giving, Koha was first developed for libraries in New Zealand. Today, Koha is used by thousands of libraries worldwide.

With access to the Koha code, our team was able to make changes to better serve our library needs. One custom change was a simplified card catalog interface. Chad Billman, Penn Manor's systems engineer, altered the default Koha search page to be easier for students to navigate, not something we could have done with a proprietary software system.

The conversion from Follett to Koha started with a pilot test at Central Manor Elementary School in April 2010. School Librarian Kathy Ashworth and Library Assistant Teresa Reisinger[20] worked side-by-side with my team to test Koha's functionality. While Chad worked on the core system, Shawn Beard coordinated the conversion of our library book records with a helpful team from Nucsoft OSSLabs, a firm based in India that specializes in Koha hosting and data migration.

During the Koha migration, Penn Manor made its first contribution to the open source community. Teresa noticed a bug in the prefilled book check-in date. Chad investigated the bug, wrote a fix for the problem, and submitted the patch to the Koha developers mailing list. Unfortunately, another programmer had already written a patch to correct the issue. Still, we were happy to reach out and make an attempt.

Of course, there were bumps during the migration, but the initial success at Central Manor Elementary demonstrated that Koha would be a fit for our other nine schools. During the summer of 2010, Penn Manor library staff trained on the new system while the tech team further refined and tuned Koha for launch. When students arrived in late August 2010, Koha was up and running in our ten school buildings.

Koha saved Penn Manor more than $50,000. It helped us build a system customized to student and teacher needs. And it closed the book on closed source commercial library systems.

Software Cost Savings

A do-it-yourself attitude and open source software saved Penn Manor a considerable amount of money. Before we leave this chapter, let's summarize the cost savings. My estimates reflect cost-avoidance of proprietary software and hardware as well as ongoing software support subscriptions. Technology personnel is required to install and maintain both commercial and open source software. Therefore, salary figures are not included.

Linux Operating System for Servers: 2001 to 2016
$75,000 - 15 years at $5,000/year

Custom Build Computer Program: 2001 to 2004
$120,000 versus finished goods and systems

Lettergrade Gradebook: 2001 to 2005
$100,000 saved from beta partnership, and open source software

Moodle Learning Management System: 2003 to 2016
$325,000 - 13 years at $25,000/year[21]

WordPress websites for students and buildings: 2008 to 2016
$160,000 - Eight years at $20,000/year[22]

Koha Library System: 2010 to 2016
$110,000 - $50,000 purchase plus $10,000/year[23]

The bottom line? $890,000 in total cost avoidance and savings. And the savings will continue to compound every year the district relies on free and open source software. However, there is more to come. When Linux and open source software moved from the server room to the classroom, the savings grew—and our students soared.

3
An Open Technology Team

So far we've seen the impact of open source software and the principles of collaboration and community on teaching and learning. I've outlined several of Penn Manor's open source learning platforms and systems. Classroom and student stories resume in the next chapter. But first, I'd like to tell you about Penn Manor's technology team and our use of open source software for enterprise communications and operations. This chapter is predominately for technology leadership and for those who are curious about our infrastructure and how my team is organized. The story of how we launched Linux laptops in our classrooms begins in the next chapter.

Meet the Techs

Penn Manor's technology secret is not hidden away in a server room or cloistered behind a firewall. Our secret is our people. The Penn Manor Technology Team is a collection of experts who love students, love learning, and are passionate about open technology. I have tremendous respect and admiration for my team's dedication, their impressive technical work, and inventiveness. They believe in education and open source values.

Cultivating a collaborative and highly productive team does not happen without mistakes and missteps. I've learned—the hard way—that technical dexterity or raw genius does not supplant dedication to an organization's mission and values. Hiring a superstar who is uninspired by a school's purpose and principles typically results in a bad situation for the candidate, and for the school. As long as a member of your team has talent, aptitude, and attitude, you can continually improve his or her skills. But when your team member is fundamentally at odds with your school's purpose, no amount of coaching will improve his or her performance.

As a school district leader, my most important job is hiring the best people. Interviewing for a spot on the Penn Manor Technology Team is a multi-day process replete with numerous problem-solving and skill challenges. I strive to recruit excellent staff via rigorous review procedures, but I'm equally mindful to select talent whose values align with the mission of public education and our do-it-yourself open source philosophy.

As of 2016, the team includes 11 full-time staff. Five technology specialists support 10 school buildings, with one dedicated full-time to Penn Manor High School's 1,725 students. Four individuals each offer specialized support for teacher professional development, the one-to-one student help desk, data systems, and department program assistance.

Chad Billman and Shawn Beard form the core of our enterprise operations and network infrastructure. Chad is a system engineer who manages wireless, data center servers, and system administration. Shawn serves as Assistant Director for Operations. Shawn has management oversight for building technology staff, as well as engineering responsibility for enterprise networking.

I report to the superintendent and serve as a member of the senior district leadership team. My primary role is to develop instructional technology strategy and learning programs. I also oversee technology infrastructure, data services, and staff professional development. Leading technology in a large public school district can be as challenging as in a large multi-dimensional organization. School technology budgets are lean, staffing is sparse, and the project list continually grows. My team manages more than 4500 student devices across 10 school buildings as well as nearly 1,000 assorted staff devices spanning multiple departments and grade levels. Our engineers support a sophisticated data center with dozens of locally hosted applications. From math to music software, and interactive boards to Internet routing, we make it all work.

Given our precious few human and fiscal resources, Penn Manor IT staff must band together to accomplish our educational mission and classroom technology goals. Necessity and scarcity force us to work smart. But without collaboration and trust, we would drown.

Values and Principles

Together, the Penn Manor Technology Team created a set of guiding principles and values that everyone agreed to uphold as golden rules. The principles and values are measurable, which helps us create metrics and markers for progress toward goals. They provide a strategic lens to help focus decisions and set direction. As a team, we:

- Focus on innovative solutions that have the greatest impact on student academic success.
- Create high-quality, individualized customer experiences that are accurate, reliable, and timely.
- Establish equipment life-cycle policies that balance current technology with fiscal responsibility.
- Act ethically and professionally to create a safe, secure, and reliable technology environment.
- Value self-sufficiency via enterprise-class, open source solutions and continually seek alternatives to closed source, proprietary systems.

Notice that last bullet point? It wasn't just me slipping in a line because I'm an open source aficionado. My team believes open source promotes technological freedom and adds value to student learning and school operations. For Jason Sauders, district building technologist, open source principles signify "a sense of humanity between every single individual by acting as a unified medium for collaboration, and the ability to contribute to any cause by the power of your voice and actions. In education, this philosophy is essential, as no singular concept, whether programming or academic practice, stands to be perfect."

Alex Lagunas, Penn Manor High School's technologist, believes the open source philosophy is fundamental to a diverse education community: "Open source allows people to transcend tribalism and belong to a true cosmopolitan community resolute on the improvement of life standards through all-inclusive access to technology. The use of open source in our schools benefits the community through the growth of its user base. This base is in constant renewal when new generations of students enter our school population every year. All these students will carry in their minds, at the very least, the awareness of the usefulness of open source; many of them will carry over to their professional careers such awareness. We are truly seeding the open source mentality in our community."

An open team is more than open source software. It's not about installing Linux on a server or slapping a hipster programming sticker on your laptop and shouting "We're Open!" Open teams operate differently from traditional top-down hierarchies. Purpose and mission often trumps precedent. Individual autonomy is heightened, as is the freedom for individuals to participate in decision-making and collective problem-solving. In his 2015 book, The Open Organization, Red Hat CEO Jim Whitehurst describes how leading effective open teams in an open organization requires a new mindset, "As CEO, I can't simply send orders down the ranks and expect everyone to jump on board. In order to drive engagement and collaboration to the roots of an organization, you need to get people involved in the decision-making process."[24]

Penn Manor's IT personnel are smart, self-directed, and energetic. Traditional command-and-control leadership does not maximize their talents, and frankly, would not serve our school district. I trust my team and provide support for their local decisions. Of course, there are times when I must direct staff to complete specific tasks. However, my role is that of chief communicator, coach, and mentor.

Penn Manor IT staff have considerable liberty and professional space to make decisions in the best interest of their assigned school buildings. They frequently collaborate with principals on grade-level initiatives, equipment allocations, and local technology programs. Building technologists spend most of their time in school buildings, but they do not directly report to the principal. To get results, teamwork is essential.

I expect the team to iterate and improvise, and encourage innovation at the micro-level. Job titles do not define the boundaries of their work. One example is teacher professional development. Building technologists conduct individualized sessions based on a teacher's need—they are not exclusively beholden to a prescribed program decreed by central administration or me.

Network Infrastructure

My team supports all areas of district technology and we work to create exceptional support experiences, reliable networks, and open learning classrooms. Central to this mission is the management and support of superior technology infrastructure. Whether it is servers, networks, hardware, routers, or telecommunications, the Penn Manor IT Team handles 95 percent of all technology infrastructure work in-house.

Chad and Shawn support more than 30 district servers. Linux servers and open source programs power 90 percent of our data center. All Internet facing servers run either Ubuntu or CentOS. Web applications are based on the LAMP stack. Server infrastructure is virtualized, which provides high availability of core services and reductions in power utilization. Most server backups occur nightly. Critical systems, such as the student management system and HR/Payroll system, receive backups and data replication on an hourly basis. Virtual server snapshotting is part of our disaster planning procedures.

All district buildings are interconnected via a 1Gbps private Ethernet network provided by Comcast Business Services. Schools have CAT5e and CAT6 structured cabling and 1Gig switched fiber backbones. The district offers classroom and office wireless connectivity via Meraki wireless N and AC access points. Community members are welcome to join the district guest wireless network, password free, when visiting Penn Manor school buildings.

Unlike most schools in the Commonwealth of Pennsylvania, Penn Manor does not contract with the local Intermediate Unit—an educational services agency—for Internet service. The district has a unique technology partnership with its academic neighbor, Millersville University of Pennsylvania. In the summer of 2000, the district installed fiber optic cabling between Penn Manor High School and the Millersville University campus. MU provided high-speed Internet access for the entire school district for more than a decade. In 2015, the district leveraged the university fiber infrastructure to light a 1GB Internet circuit to the Keystone Initiative for Network Based Education and Research (KINBER), an academic network consortium for Pennsylvania schools and colleges. Our university partnership efforts and in-house network expertise have saved us about $250,000 in network and Internet Service Provider connectivity charges over the past 15 years.

IRC and Mattermost

Penn Manor is a big place. With ten buildings and a 113-square-mile geographical footprint, coordination and communication can be challenging. Getting my team together in the same physical place at the same time is not always possible. And during those rare times when a server is offline or a recalcitrant network switch is acting out, keeping everyone abreast of the situation is essential. Two open source tools have been indispensable for our communication needs: Internet Relay Chat (IRC) and, more recently, a private Mattermost server.

If you work outside the technology industry, you may not be familiar with IRC. It is one of the earliest open Internet communication tools for live text-based chat. IRC is organized around real-time group discussion forums, typically called channels. If you have ever participated in an online chat of any kind, from AOL to Skype, you have a good idea of what IRC chats are like. Use of IRC has declined over the past 10 years, largely due to the rise of Twitter and other social media sites. Nonetheless, programmers and system administrators love it. Public IRC networks, like the 85,000 member Freenode[25] system, are popular destinations for both software developers and those seeking software help. If you need a hand with open source software, you will likely find a friendly guide on Freenode IRC.

IRC server software has evolved into dozens of variants. For years, Penn Manor's self-hosted IRC server ran Dancer-IRCD. My team maintained three channel rooms, each with a slightly different discussion focus. The #helpdesk channel was our main discussion room. Conversations about Puppet—our configuration management software for student laptops—happened in a room called, simply, #puppet. Random discussions about technology news took place in the #swimmingpool channel.

To talk on an IRC network, you need an IRC software client. Our team typically uses HexChat—which runs on Linux, Mac OS X, and Windows—and LimeChat for Mac OS X. I recommend both HexChat and LimeChat if you are just getting started with IRC.

One downside to IRC is the interface. It hasn't changed much since I graduated high school in 1990. For programmers who spend lots of time on a command line, IRC is terrific. But teachers and students are accustomed to chat apps with modern graphic interfaces. Plus, accessing past IRC discussion history can be cumbersome. IRC is designed to be a real-time board. Once you close an IRC client, you miss the conversation while you are away. We maneuvered around this limitation with an IRC program that archived our chat transcripts. But by late 2015, my team sought a more flexible solution, and I wanted to expand the system to students and teachers.

Google Hangouts was a possible replacement; so was a platform called Slack. Slack had great features, but at $12 per account per year, Penn Manor would pay over $12,000 annually. Plus, Slack's terms of service did not permit children under 18 to use the software.[26] And we wanted an open source solution running on internal district servers, not Software as a Service storing Penn Manor conversations on someone else's system. In January 2016, we selected an emerging program called Mattermost.[27]

Mattermost is an open source instant messaging, chat, notification, and communication board all rolled into one system. Mattermost uses a private team concept. Every team starts with a general discussion channel called #TownHall. We added our standard IT channel topics: #HelpDesk, #Puppet, #BugHunt, and a few others. Since it is open source, and extensible, Chad wrote a program to send new support ticket notifications into the Mattermost #HelpDesk channel, just like we had in our previous IRC system.[28]

Mattermost supports direct messages, emoji characters, embedded pictures and shared files. Conversation history persists inside the discussion channel. We can scroll back through the chat history and read pass messages, just like a Skype or IM discussion. When we step away from the Mattermost screen, we receive email notifications when our name appears in a discussion.

All conversations—even private direct conversations—are logged and accessible for review. And with our servers onsite, we ensure a degree of seclusion and confidentiality that public networks can't offer.

Unlike email, Mattermost is a convenient virtual meeting room and a central dashboard for district technology operations. I was incredibly fond of our internal IRC system, but I love the Mattermost platform. It costs nothing more than a little server space and occasional software update attention. But even better, it has become a communication hub for our Student Help Desk and allowed our apprentices to communicate and collaborate when they are not together in the same physical class location.

Can You Hear Me Now?

Online chat rooms are convenient, but sometimes you need to pick up the phone and call a colleague. If you are a school or business IT leader, you are well aware that commercial phone systems cost a fortune. The bill for desk phones, PBX controllers, licensing, and support can be shocking. And once you buy a proprietary phone system, you're locked in with that vendor for the long haul.

And what if a third party acquires your phone system provider? Will the new company support your existing system, or will your PBX become a dusty metal box on a slow march to the scrap heap? I found myself wrangling with this exact problem in the spring of 2010.

For years, Penn Manor used phones and equipment manufactured by 3COM. In the summer of 2007, we completed a multi-year district-wide installation of a 3COM NBX phone system. My team was excited to finish the installation, which started with the Letort Elementary School renovation project in 2001. Every classroom now had a modern Voice Over IP (VoIP) phone system. Phone system upgrades are long-term investments, right? Well, not this one.

In November 2009, HP announced it would acquire 3COM. By April 2010, 3COM no longer existed as a separate company. Bad news soon arrived: HP announced that no NBX phones, controllers or licenses would be available for purchase after July 30, 2010. HP would focus development on the 3COM VCX phone platform. Then, in January 2011,

HP announced that the VCX phone system would be entering maintenance mode—no new updates were coming. The following year, HP cut the cord on the VCX system.[29]

My long-term phone platform strategy was suddenly looking pretty short-term. With the NBX product end of life, we couldn't access vendor support or purchase the proprietary software licenses required to add new phones. My concern was student and staff welfare because a voice system is vital to school safety. We were in a jam, but the alternative proprietary communication systems from vendors like Avaya, Cisco, and Microsoft were prohibitively expensive to implement. Neighboring school districts with 3COM phones began moving to other proprietary solutions. We wanted freedom from vendor control.

Shawn headed up the search for a replacement system and ultimately recommended sipXcom, an open source voice and unified communications voice platform.[30] Thousands of enterprises, including Amazon and Red Hat, as well as numerous university systems, had implemented sipXcom for global voice communications. We were attracted to the robust community of developers and encouraged by the adoption by other major organizations. If Amazon was using sipXcom, it should be a reliable solution for our classrooms.

An open source, standards-based phone server provided another advantage: No longer would we be married to a proprietary desk phone. The sipXcom software worked with phones from a variety of manufacturers. We decided to use Polycom IP phones, which were less than half the price of the proprietary 3COM NBX phones.

Shawn and the team first installed the sipXcom platform at Letort Elementary School in April 2012, approximately 10 years after the building received the first 3COM VoIP PBX system. Letort teachers were also the first in our district to receive the Polycom Soundpoint IP phones. Outside callers noticed little difference. But we knew it was a success when teachers dryly remarked, "It's a phone. I dial numbers and get voicemail. What else is there to say?"

Other school building staff and teachers echoed the same low-key sentiment during the three-year transition to the sipXcom/Polycom system. In December 2015, Penn Manor High School was the last building to be upgraded. Staff and teachers were happy. My team was happy, and our taxpayers were happy as well. We've saved at least $250,000 by choosing the open source sipXcom platform. And again, the district is no longer encumbered with expensive and risky proprietary vendor systems.

Backing Up Isn't Hard to Do

Phones are rather boring when you think about them. That is, if you even think about them. Calling from a desk phone to the school front office doesn't rank at the top of anyone's list of thrilling daily tasks. However, they are essential for school communications. You'd miss them if they were gone, especially in an emergency situation.

File backups are about as exciting as phones. I bet you wouldn't cancel a hot date to stay inside and back up files on a Friday night. But I suspect you would miss your data files if they ran off in the middle of the night.

Educators are usually preoccupied with more interesting and pressing affairs than data backups. For a second-grade teacher, finding 30 seconds for a bathroom break is more urgent than sorting out a backup strategy. Teacher restroom logistics are still a work in progress, but in the summer of 2013, my team solved the backup problem with a free and open source tool called Nextcloud.[31]

Nextcloud is an automatic file backup and synchronization server. If you have used commercial programs like Dropbox or Microsoft OneDrive, you're familiar with the concept. A little client application runs on your laptop and automatically copies files to a server. Your files are stored on both your local computer and your Nextcloud server folder. Should your hot date inadvertently set your school laptop on fire, duplicates of all your lesson plan documents live on inside the Nextcloud server.

The Nextcloud client runs on Linux, Mac, Windows, Android, and iOS. It silently watches for additions and changes to a designated folder. When a lesson plan file changes, the client duplicates the updated file to the server. This process happens without any intervention; we set it and forget about it. I've lost count of how many times Nextcloud saved staff data files from mundane hard drive crashes and spectacular liquid spills.

Documents and files stored on Nextcloud are available via the web. The web interface includes document sharing and collaborative editing tools similar to Google Docs. As of 2016, the collaborative editing capabilities are still evolving, but the features improve with each subsequent release. Ultimately, Nextcloud may become a private alternative to Google Docs.

We run Nextcloud on GlusterFS, Red Hat's robust open source storage file system. The setup handles on-premise storage and sync services for more than 500 school employees. Staff, teacher, and administrative data files are secure on private, internal district servers. Data mining, surveillance, and third-party sharing of sensitive data force teachers to dodge a ghastly spitball of tangled student privacy issues. With Nextcloud, we control access to confidential student files and rest assured that a third-party software vendor isn't mining student data for fun and profit.

Supporting a private cloud means my team is responsible for server infrastructure, data integrity, and security monitoring. It is a challenge we readily accept in return for freedom from commercial vendor lock-in. But Nextcloud can be a small-scale solution too. Students and teachers could set up a classroom Nextcloud server using a Raspberry Pi. Wouldn't that be a cool project at your school?

The Open Secret

Colleagues ask me, "How do you achieve your system savings? How did you pull this off? What's the secret to overcoming the resistance?" They're typically surprised by my answer: Hire passionate talent, trust them, and be a mentor. It sounds so basic. It sounds so contrived. It almost sounds like a provocation, but it's the essence of a great organization and a great school.

It takes time, and sometimes many mistakes, to develop an effective process for bringing the right people onboard and for creating the environment a team needs to do its best work. Stellar teams don't sprout because a manager waves a magic wand and sprinkles buzzword glitter. Innovation and growth emerge from within teams and between colleagues. Performance is the product of individual strength, passion, and relationships. When you trust passionate and smart people to innovate, and provide the resources to make it happen, they will find amazing solutions to difficult problems.

In this chapter, we explored my team's open source culture, systems, and communication tools. At the beginning of the chapter, I said that my most important job as an IT manager is to hire the best talent and coach them to grow professionally. As a school leader, my most important job is to inspire students to change the world. The following chapters are stories about how the open source model has empowered students and transformed learning in the Penn Manor School District. Our destination is the Penn Manor High School one-to-one laptop program and Student Help Desk. But the journey begins in our elementary schools.

4
Linux is Elementary

In 2010, the elementary school laptop fleet was torn and frayed. The incongruous collection of iBook G3 and G4 laptops approached eight years old. In computer years, they were born during the medieval era. It was past time for laptop upgrades.

Of course, budgets mattered. In 2010, Pennsylvania schools faced an astronomical climb in employee pension contribution costs. The pension problem was the result of a 2001 legislative decision to increase public employee pension benefits, including benefits to the legislators. A massive loss of investment funds, due to a weak stock market, followed. Local school districts had to shoulder the burden of covering the resulting funding gap. Penn Manor School District—and every other public school system in Pennsylvania—faced serious fiscal issues due to legislative decisions completely out of the control of local school boards.

Internally, our leadership discussions centered on the damage budgetary cuts would inflict on staffing and programs. As a cost-cutting measure, we trimmed the annual district technology budget by $100,000, a 33 percent decrease. It wasn't good news, but the alternative could have been reductions in teaching staff, art and music instruction, or curtailments in other student programs.

In the middle of the fiscal crisis, I was challenged to replace elementary school laptops and to provide the greatest number of classroom computers at the lowest cost. By this time, elementary classroom technology use was finally growing. My annual staff and faculty technology services survey revealed teachers strongly identified three critical instructional technology needs: more tech support staff, more time for professional development, and more classroom computers.

Teachers recognized technology was a crucial part of their daily instruction, but we couldn't afford to upgrade our old Apple laptops.

Free and open source software was at the center of district IT operations, but classroom computers were another matter entirely. Penn Manor's elementary schools had predominately used Mac desktops and laptops since the turn of the century. During the 2010-2011 academic year, a visitor would have observed Apple iBooks in the hands of teachers and in scores of classrooms. Most computers were housed in laptop carts, with one cart for each of the district's seven elementary schools.

The iBook laptops in the aging fleet were a mix of models and vintages. Various models were purchased over the course of several years as funds were available from both Penn Manor Education Foundation grants and the district technology budget. Carts had two, and often three or more, different models in the mix. When a cart rolled into a classroom, students were heard whispering the technology wish "G4, G4, G4!" as they opened the lid. If the logo revealed the imprint of a slower-generation laptop, sadness prevailed.

Replacing each Apple iBook with a current MacBook would have been, at a minimum, $900 per laptop. But the hardware price was not the only cost. Additional productivity software, such as Microsoft Office, and software to remotely manage the laptops would cost extra. The total acquisition price for an Apple laptop would be approximately $1000 per unit.

Teachers wanted additional student laptops. With huge needs, I needed to think differently. I needed to find a low-cost, effective, and sustainable solution.

A Different Path

I know this book is about school technology but, before continuing, I must be crystal clear about the value of teachers. Technology becomes tired and obsolete quickly, but the impact of an inspiring teacher can transcend the boundaries of a student's school career and create learning ripples across a lifetime. Teaching is about relationships with students, not technology. There's nothing more to say here, folks.

In the hands of open-minded teachers, technology is intellectual rocket fuel. Of course, not all devices will launch students into the learning stratosphere. Overhead projectors and filmstrip projectors were long considered essential instructional devices for classrooms. But I suspect few of us would say that the overhead projector itself kindled career ambitions to become an artist or astronaut.

Computers are, of course, more capable than filmstrip projectors. Modern computers are seemingly infinite communication, creation, and learning kits tuned for the multiplicity of human intellectual expression. Try writing a symphony, sequencing DNA, or analyzing the impact of rising global temperatures on anything less than a modern computer.

School technology is about products. And technology products are tied to advertising and marketing. Consider how companies such as Apple, Google, Microsoft, and Samsung invoke emotion to cajole us into purchasing their wares. Their advertisements are carefully crafted to sell feelings of happiness, power, and acceptance. They can manipulate our purchasing behaviors with feelings of fear. Our purchasing behavior is often based on feelings, not facts or figures.[32] If the marketing teams at Apple, Google, and Microsoft are effective, they will have silenced the rational, analytical part of our brains, and amplified our emotional associations with a glowing gadget. Walk the vendor floor of education conferences sponsored by the International Society for Educational Technology or the National School Board Association for proof. You'll find no shortage of companies offering to ease a principal's angst by way of an enchanting technology box alleged to make students more proficient 21st century learners—whatever that means.

I've witnessed many school leaders purchase technology based on emotion and group-think, rather than thoughtful reflection and a guiding philosophy on what students will be able to do with a given device. However, it's not difficult to understand why well-meaning administrators and school boards make such impulsive decisions. A loquacious list of nerdy tech specs, stats, and lingo define the devices we want to buy. It's just so much easier to purchase the same familiar Apple or Microsoft stuff. Besides, the companies advertise themselves as friends to education! Writing a symphony? Real musicians use Macs to do that! Sequencing DNA? Everyone knows Windows is a scientist's best friend!

When the perception is that every school in the country is buying Apple, Google, or Microsoft products, wandering from the flock can be risky. In the fall of 2010, while my team and I were thinking about which device to purchase for elementary classrooms, the national school technology herd was stampeding toward either Apple's iPad or traditional Windows laptops. It was in this context, and with the support of Penn Manor's Superintendent, Dr. Mike Leichliter, that I began an open dialogue with teachers and staff about the necessity of purchasing less costly alternatives to MacBooks so we could achieve the goal of increasing student access to technology.

Linux on the Desktop

If we were to seriously consider PC laptops as cost effective alternatives to Apple devices, why not also evaluate Linux as an alternative to the standard Microsoft Windows and Office duo? Even in 2010, nearly two decades after its creation, Linux still didn't receive the same coverage in the U.S. education press enjoyed by Apple, Google, or Microsoft. But Linux was far from a fringe operating system. Besides being the core software behind the Internet, Linux was alive and well in thousands of schools, businesses, and organizations worldwide. Linux distributions like Ubuntu, an operating system tuned specifically for desktop use, had matured into perfectly usable day-to-day systems for classroom computing.

From a strictly financial standpoint, Linux on student laptops would sidestep the costs of purchasing an operating system and word-processing suite. We'd also dodge the need to buy anti-virus software. Linux was, and is today, immune to the thousands of malware programs and security issues common to Microsoft Windows. If we avoided software fees, the savings could help us buy more classroom laptops or give us the option to route the funds to other district programs.

Linux may have been a new concept for Penn Manor laptops, but it wasn't a new concept to education. The use of Linux in schools was rising, thanks to the growing adoption of netbooks, and the need to trim budgets.[33] Likewise, successful large-scale deployments in the U.S. and Europe proved Linux was a match for classrooms. Two notable implementations were Saugus Union School District in California and Littleton Public Schools in Colorado. Both had used Linux powered laptops as part of district-wide student writing initiatives since 2008.[34] Overseas, it was easy to find many examples of schools adopting Linux, including a mammoth 220,000-computer implementation across 2,000 schools in Andalusia, Spain.[35]

Pinching pennies wasn't the only motivation for considering Linux. Our students deserved versatile learning machines for a full range of activities. The device ought to have a great web experience for Google Docs, which was rapidly being adopted by teachers. Faculty relied on educational websites running Flash. The usual word processing and presentation tools had to be there too. And we needed a machine that students could use for creative audio and video production, programming, and art. Any device or operating system that couldn't provide fundamental classroom necessities would be off the list, no matter how inexpensive it might be.

The Great Tablet Debate

As I was gathering feedback from teachers and principals about our next technology refresh, an intense debate about devices was raging inside the Penn Manor IT Team. Some were adamant that elementary classrooms receive iPads, and no other device should be considered, let alone Linux and open source software. Although strategic educational technology decisions are my call, I've always encouraged open and frank dialogue with my staff. My process for this decision was no different.

The tablet proponents endorsed their position with unvarnished passion and emotion. It was a tense time for the team. The experience underscored how critical it is to have people working toward the same organizational values and goals. In spite of the disharmony, I asked all of my staff to engage and provide open and constructive input. Everyone deserved a chance to be heard.

Apple's iPad transfixed many in the educational technology community. It had debuted with much fanfare and glamor in January 2010. By the fall of 2010, it was the darling of the educational technology press. When first released, the consumer price for a 16GB model was $499. Pricing for schools was $475—not much of a discount for education. The cost was less than a MacBook laptop, but an iPad wasn't a laptop either. For $500, or less, we could buy capable PC laptops.

Cost comparisons aside, the iPad presented serious support challenges. Efficient fleet-management software tools didn't exist. The iPad paradigm was that of a one-owner mobile device, with personal apps, purchased via a personal credit card. Few fourth-graders were walking into school with a Mastercard in hand. Apple offered a volume purchase program for apps, but the circuitous and cumbersome procurement process was frustrating early adopters.[36] We concluded iPads were not ideal for the shared-use model in our classrooms.

Furthermore, iPad's absence of Flash was a significant roadblock. Back then, countless educational websites relied on Flash for multimedia playback. Even today, in 2016, my team wrangles with support requests related to websites using Flash. Rolling out a device without Flash would have forced teachers to scramble needlessly for alternate curriculum resources.

Early on, iPad file workflow was muddled. The device was designed to be a single user tool; student-to-student and student-to-teacher collaboration was severely limited. Exactly how would teachers get files to the iPad, and in turn, how would students submit files back to teachers? The iPad favored cloud services, like Dropbox, for sharing.

However, many of the cloud-based services restricted use by children under the age of 13. Email might be an option for teachers, but distributing, collecting, and organizing droves of student files via email was undesirable.

Functional concerns aside, I was troubled by the iPad's closed nature. The essence of the device was about control. You couldn't, and can't, upgrade or replace components. The physical and digital hoods were welded shut, and with that, a student's ability to examine, study, and build upon the underlying technology. The operating system was inaccessible. It was the ultimate read-only gadget. Everything that made computing powerful for learners was gone. What was this thing?

It became apparent this new gadget was the supreme consumer consumption device. The only way to add capabilities (software) to an iPad is via a shopping trip to the Apple App Store, a marketplace controlled by a single company. Never had a computing device so boldly denigrated the power of computing and the spirit of making. If this device represented the future of educational technology, as some pundits prophesied, kids would not be better off. I could not impose the limitations of the iPad on our students.

To be clear, I don't abhor tablets. My team supports iPads for special needs students who require iOS specific apps. We've deployed and supported approximately 150 Android-powered Nexus tablets across multiple grade levels. About 200 Penn Manor teachers carry district-issued Samsung tablets. However, in every case, a tablet is not the sole computing device. Students and teachers still use laptops as their primary technology device. Even today, no staff have agreed to trade their district-issued laptop to use a tablet exclusively.

As my team spent more time with Linux, it became clear that the operating system could serve as a foundation for classroom computing. On January 22, 2011, I ended the device debate with an email to my staff. After careful consideration of teacher needs, cost, and district educational goals, I decided to move forward with a plan to provide the elementary schools with laptops running Linux. It would be a platform shift for our students and teachers, but I was confident it was the best decision for our students. They would benefit from updated systems and have more access to learning technology. I was excited to get started on the project.

One More Data Point

As the Linux plan moved forward, Chad Billman emailed the team with an insightful discovery. Chad used a program called Casper, a commercial software tool we used to manage Mac laptops, to uncover the amount of time each desktop application was in use on student laptops. The Casper report yielded a detailed profile of classroom activity on the student iBooks, and it disclosed statistics unavailable through teacher self-reporting or classroom observations.

Chad was characteristically impartial as he presented the unexpected finding: During the previous month, approximately 85 percent of all elementary student computing time was spent using the Firefox web browser. About 10 percent of student time was spent in standard office suite programs, mostly Word and PowerPoint with a smattering of Apple's Pages software. The remaining five percent of computing time was spent idle or in utility programs like Preview. Students almost never launched audio and video software like Garage Band and iMovie.

Web access, word processing, and slideware. That was the limit of the student computing experience. The numbers told a bittersweet story. We would have been better served, financially, with much less of a laptop during the preceding years. The laptops were essentially used as Chromebooks before the Chromebook was even cool.[37]

Laptop Shopping

With an operating system strategy set, we immersed ourselves in gear. The switch to PC laptops opened a vast constellation of hardware for our review. We researched battery life, keyboard comfort, physical size, screen size, toughness (because, elementary students!), and, of course, price. The bombardment of devices, spec sheets, features, and options would probably have induced nausea for most. I was thrilled to have so many choices.

We reviewed netbooks, the lightweight low-power laptops that were something of a precursor to Google's Chromebook. Although inexpensive and lightweight, the Atom processors typically found in netbooks proved too sluggish. A leading contender was "Frank," our peculiar codename for Dell's 13" Vostro laptop. Frank fared well in classroom testing, but the price hovered around $500, and we needed to do better. Then, in early January 2011, Lenovo introduced the new x120e laptop at the Consumer Electronics Show in Las Vegas. Early reviews were excellent—it was a Best in Show award winner—and the features looked good. A demo was on the way.

Lenovo's X120e was a lightweight 11.6 inch laptop, weighing about three pounds. It was sturdy and not too big for young students. The full keyboard was comfy. We liked the anti-glare matte screen finish and the screen's ability to lay nearly flat without stressing the hinges. The laptop had an Ethernet port (useful for connecting to a network) and both VGA and HDMI projector ports. The x120e used AMD's Fusion chip, which was energy efficient. Battery life was about 6 hours, enough to get through a school day.

Classroom demos of the Lenovo laptop confirmed my team's positive impressions. In May 2011, I ordered 620 Lenovo x120e laptops. The final price was $385 per laptop. We ordered 2.5 laptops for the price of one MacBook. Each elementary school would receive two mobile laptop carts, with 30 laptops per cart. And since we were under budget, I purchased additional laptops for use in middle and high school classrooms.

The Distribution and the Desktop

As the search for the best student laptop progressed, my team was working to select and refine the Linux operating system for our students. Our goal was simple: present an easy-to-use desktop uniquely tuned to elementary student needs. This shift required thoughtful planning. If the Linux desktop looked like a tangle of weird buttons and freakish behaviors, teachers would be jarred by the new technology.

Windows is a prefabricated operating system with a concrete graphical user interface (GUI). Microsoft preselects the location of the Start menu, how folders open and close, what icons look like, and little system behaviors that make the Windows desktop feel like, well, Windows. It may be possible to adjust some settings, but Microsoft's makes it difficult to significantly alter the desktop. Apple's OS X follows a similar design philosophy—the desktop is bolted into the underlying computer system. If you get a Mac, you get Apple's desktop, no exceptions.

No desktop shotgun marriages happen in the Linux world. Linux is built on open, modular software building blocks. The mixing and matching of desktops and system distributions is common and encouraged. Global communities of Linux developers and designers have brewed hundreds of distributions with hundreds of desktop variations. Developers create distributions to suit the tastes and needs of users. Distro Astro is crafted for astronomy enthusiasts. Fedora aims to be free of all proprietary code. Arch Linux ascribes to a minimalist philosophy.

The diversity of Linux distributions gives schools options. My team focused on distributions with wide-scale support and long-term maintenance. Two companies were leaders in the development and support of enterprise-grade Linux distributions. Canonical, based in London, develops and maintains Ubuntu. Red Hat, with corporate headquarters in Raleigh, North Carolina, develops CentOS, Fedora, and Red Hat Enterprise Linux.

We selected the Ubuntu Linux distribution for several reasons. Chad and Shawn had collected years of technical experience with Ubuntu on district servers. Their Linux server skills and knowledge would transfer to the student laptops. However, Ubuntu was more than just a cryptic server system. Gone were the days of sifting through obscure technical guides to get Linux running. Ubuntu had developed into an easy-to-use replacement for Mac OS X and Windows.

Another decisive factor was the pace at which the operating system would need to be upgraded to a newer version. Typically, an upgrade becomes essential when a vendor stops providing software security updates. At the time, many Linux distributions embraced either a rolling release schedule, where they update core components of the operating system, or a fast release schedule, where the entire system becomes outdated in 12 to 16 months.

Every two years, Canonical releases an Ubuntu reference update that is guaranteed to receive critical bug fixes, updates, and security patches. Called a long-term support (LTS) release, it includes support for up to five years. Since our initial roll out would be a pilot, we agreed to use the then-current version of Ubuntu, 11.04, while planning to rebuild our software master image on the forthcoming LTS release (12.04) in the spring of 2012.

Linux has historically been well supported on Lenovo laptops, but the x120e laptop was a new product. Some software drivers worked as soon as we installed Ubuntu; others needed debugging. For example, the laptop's Realtek wireless card required a newer software driver than the one included in Ubuntu 11.04. The laptop also needed a few minor behind-the-scenes tweaks to make it perform smoothly. Chad handily tackled these setup and configuration tasks and helped push our Linux project along.

GNOME or Xfce

Security, stability, and drivers were important to my team, but students and teachers just wanted a computer that worked and had an elegant desktop. Unmoored from the Mac OS X dock, and with the Start button well behind us, it was time to design the Penn Manor student laptop desktop. One option was GNOME, a desktop interface common to Linux.[38] Much like Mac OS X and Windows, GNOME uses familiar desktop features. GNOME looked good, but in the spring of 2011, Canonical announced a new desktop interface project called Unity.

Unity was an ambitious rework of the Ubuntu desktop. Reception to early beta versions was all over the map. Aesthetic opinion aside, Unity was clearly a work in progress, and much of the visual polish was years away. Furthermore, Unity ran best on more powerful computer systems. This presented a bit of a conundrum for my team. The x120e laptop was a capable machine, but not a processing powerhouse. To keep costs low and to increase battery life, we opted for a less burly, and power-hungry, CPU and graphics chip. Future Unity software updates might cause the laptops to run slow.

However, with Linux we had options. We could substitute a desktop interface better suited for our students. Chad suggested an alternative interface called Xfce.[39] His idea stuck, even if the name didn't roll off the tongue.

The Xfce desktop interface combines friendly graphics with light system requirements. It runs remarkably well on low-cost hardware and can be used to revive older computers that can no longer run Windows. An Xfce desktop is minimal. Graphics and menus are sparse. But the modest first impression conceals Xfce's remarkable flexibility. We could customize every visual option: icons, colors, panels, windows, and appearance settings.

Given so many building blocks to choose from, my team could tailor the Xfce desktop based on feedback from teachers and students. Teachers helped decide the placement of the panels and cheered or sneered at button icons. And if a teacher wanted to provide pupils with quick access to a website, we could add a custom one-click button. The Xfce desktop was like a canvas on which we could paint our perfect classroom computing picture. The time and energy spent crafting a custom desktop from teacher feedback helped make the shift to a new computer platform much easier for students and staff.

Puppet Masters

One last problem remained: How would we support our new Linux laptop fleet? Security patches and upgrades were easy to manage on Linux servers because the systems ran continually and we could connect to them as needed. Student laptops posed a challenge. We didn't have a standard schedule for when the laptops would be switched on or off. And we needed to juggle software requirements that varied widely by grade level.

Chad was thinking outside of the box. He proposed Puppet[40], an open source program typically used with servers. Puppet is a configuration management utility—simply, software to manage software. A system administrator might use Puppet to change settings on dozens of servers simultaneously. Or, Puppet may be used to update 300 servers to a new software release. Puppet can scale to hundreds and even hundreds of thousands of computers. Intel, NASA, Starbucks, and Twitter use Puppet to manage immensely complex systems and websites. NASA may have been using Puppet to manage a terrestrial data center for the Mars Curiosity Rover, but our requirement was much more audacious: we needed classroom technology for students who may someday be supporting a data center on Mars.

Puppet can perform incredible feats of mass enchantment. A skilled administrator can command Puppet to configure every last application, software configuration, and user preference on a Linux system. Commands are coded and saved in text files, called Puppet manifests, holding directives for computer settings. When a laptop first boots, it checks the Puppet server for new commands, and if it finds them, acts on those orders.

With his usual intensity and laser focus, Chad dived into a period of serious self-study. After a couple of months, he resurfaced as our resident Puppet Master. Coaching the entire team to the same level of expertise also took time. During the 2011-2012 school year, Chad led the IT Team through multiple in-house training sessions or, as we called them, Puppet Jams. Brain stretches probably would have been a better description. Our building technicians found Puppet challenging at first. Ultimately, as with any form of exercise, the pain was worth the gain. My team emerged with new Puppet skills to successfully wrangle the Linux laptop fleet en masse.

Since technology staff would be asked to coordinate all sorts of laptop preferences on a classroom-by-classroom basis, the list of Puppet commands could become a tangled coil in short order. Documenting each other's work was vital. Plus, we need a quality review process to keep software bugs from crawling into the elementary laptops.

Chad brought order to the potential chaos by introducing a software version control system called Git.[41] Created by the father of Linux, Linus Torvalds, Git is often used by programming teams to keep everyone's code synchronized. A close analogy would be Google Docs, where multiple people can happily work and comment on the same document.

Fortunately, Chad had the foresight to begin reshaping the team's software management practices well ahead of our future open source one-to-one programs. I certainly didn't have the second sight to predict 620 Linux laptops growing to 4000 laptops in under four years.

Showtime for the Little Laptops

The grand exhibition of our work opened in August 2011. Refreshed and recharged from summer break, elementary teachers received an orientation to the new laptops during start-of-school professional development workshops. Terms like Xfce, Ubuntu, and Linux were unfamiliar, but it didn't matter. Teachers had little problem navigating the new desktops. Training didn't center on how the laptop worked. The time was spent exploring new learning possibilities.

My team preloaded dozens of free and open source learning programs: Audacity, GIMP, Google Earth, Inkscape, LibreOffice, Scratch, and Stellarium. Google Docs worked without any Linux-specific glitches. Flash and Java-enabled websites ran fine. As teachers dove in and played and became more excited about the new computers, any remaining doubts about Linux in the classroom faded.

By the end of 2011, elementary teachers had adjusted to the new technology. They regularly reached for the Linux carts for day-to-day learning activities. The Linux laptops in the middle schools were commonly used for reading interventions. A history teacher at Penn Manor High School used the laptops as part of a paperless classroom pilot program. Teachers appreciated how sturdy and rugged the devices were. We watched many laptops fall to the floor and survive, no worse for the wear. Battery life exceeded our expectations. Students made it through a full day without a recharge.

I noticed how little training and technical support was needed. So much emotion was tied up in what Linux and open source desktop could not do. Naysayers argued that the systems would limit student learning or confound teachers. We discovered no substantial educational tradeoffs with Linux. Our systems could meet and, in some cases, exceed the capabilities of Mac and Windows laptops. Students could create audio and video, and they could collaborate on projects. Applications, buttons, and icons may look a little different on a Linux system, but visual differences were no barrier to learning.

...

Many years after the initial transition to Linux laptops, I spoke with Central Manor Elementary School's fourth-grade teachers about the impact of the laptops in the elementary classrooms. We talked about the idea of reducing device costs to purchase more laptops, and they candidly shared how pervasive access to computers and the Internet was vital because not all students arrive with the same prior life experiences and knowledge.

Becca Eichler shared how the laptops helped level the playing field in her class. "We have more and more kids who don't go on vacation, and, outside of school, some don't leave their home very often. When we were recently talking about landforms and the 'coast,' some of my students said they had never visited the beach. With technology, we are able to show them pictures of where the water hits the land. They then had a visual because they didn't come to us with these experiences."

Heather Piatt shared a story about one of her timid students. "We were learning about food chains in science. One student surprised me because he is as quiet as can be, but the computer allowed him to explore and gave him more confidence. Other students perceived him in a different way—he was seen as a role model and a leader."

For Amy Wiggins, the laptops help decentralize learning, especially when a skilled teacher is willing to release some control and transfer agency to her students. "You can't be afraid to say you don't know everything," she says "The students are the facilitators. I'm no longer the teacher; there are many facilitators of technology knowledge. Instead of me taking the reins, we have 10 facilitators in the room. It's all these little spiderweb effects."

The spiderweb effect, where students have the freedom and autonomy to be technology leaders to their peers, is tremendously empowering. "For some kids, it's the time they get to shine," said teacher Laura Heverling.

Linux Learning Island

As the 2011-2012 school year progressed, our confidence with Linux and open source software increased. An opportunity to creatively apply Linux presented itself as renovations to Central Manor Elementary School wrapped up. Unlike our six other elementary buildings, we had the space and opportunity to install a dedicated computer lab. The new lab received 30 desktops running Ubuntu and open source applications.

The lab was popular with teachers and students, but a surprise discovery led to the creation of a fun learning space. During building construction, workers uncovered a large section of exquisite hardwood flooring dating back to the original school building, circa 1930. The hardwood floor was preserved and became a distinctive artifact of the renovation. For about a year, the section of the building was affectionately known as the "bowling alley" before the idea of a digital learning space began to take shape.

Several of us wanted to amplify this artifact and build an interactive and creative learning space suitable for digital presentations and small-group collaborative work. I had a sense of what the technology would be like, but the open area and handsome flooring called for special treatment and a distinctive theme.

Denny Coleman, Penn Manor's Director of Building and Grounds, and Central Manor Principal Deb Holt masterminded the ambiance. Denny designed and built an island setting complete with a mini-stage for impromptu class presentations, hanging tropical fixtures, easily movable student furniture, and artistic wall paintings. The corner space became an inviting imaginative place for students to unleash their creativity.

The Learning Island features five large LCD monitors powered by tiny Nettop PCs running Linux. Each PC is connected to the building Wi-Fi network and has a wireless keyboard with an integrated mouse. The PCs include our standard suite of open source software, which enables our students to research, write, program, and design. When needed, teachers and students can connect the classroom and cart laptops to the LCD monitors.

Technology in this learning space is pervasive, but it's not the focal point. Electronics may be stowed away when not needed. Flexibility is central to the design. The open classroom provides active, passive, and collaborative learning spaces. And teachers can configure and quickly reconfigure the space for project work, readers' theater, or whole group presentations.

From Free to Freedom

The amount of money taxpayers saved by switching to Linux and open source was incredible. At the time, 620 laptops running Linux and open source software cost $70,000 less than an implementation of iPads and $250,000 less than the price of a standard $900 MacBook. We could redirect those saving into teacher salaries, equipment, facilities and other instructional programs. Premium-priced devices from Apple would be difficult to justify when affordable and sustainable alternatives proved to be equal or better. It was not worth the expense to have a brand name on a given device. After all, education is about the student, not the logo.

With both the viability and cost savings of classroom Linux proven, it was again time to expand the elementary classroom laptop fleet. In the spring of 2012, I purchased 1,000 Lenovo x130 laptops, all slated to run Ubuntu 12.04. It was the largest laptop setup project in Penn Manor's history. Each elementary classroom would receive six new laptops running our custom Ubuntu Linux image. Desktop Linux was expanding into the middle schools as well. In March 2012, we replaced the aging iMacs in Manor Middle School's computer lab with in-house built desktop computers running Ubuntu.

At the beginning of the 2012-2013 school year, Penn Manor's total Linux computing fleet totaled 1,700 devices, the largest free and open source implementation in the state of Pennsylvania. Free and open source software offered salvation in the face of dramatic district budget cuts, and enabled us to provide more classroom technology to more students.

Little did I know that our best work was still ahead. We were initially attracted to free and open source software because of the cost savings, but ultimately, it was the spirit of open that liberated our students and opened our schoolhouse.

5
Planning a One-to-One Program

Penn Manor was preposterously late to the one-to-one school laptop party. Methodist Ladies' College—an independent girls school in Melbourne Australia—pioneered the first laptop learning program in February 1990. A decade later, the governor of the state of Maine announced an ambitious plan to give every seventh-grader a school laptop. By 2010, districts across the United States initiated large-scale one-to-one programs.[42]

Providing a laptop to every student in a large school system is not an easy feat, and for many districts, it's fiscally unattainable. Before 2012, I never imagined our district could afford to issue every middle and high school student a laptop. But now, Linux and open source software offered a solution.

In May 2012, district administrators and I talked with the school board about long-term computing plans. I outlined upcoming classroom laptop update needs during a regular technology state-of-the-union presentation. Penn Manor High School would soon need to replace 400 student MacBook laptops received via the 2007 Pennsylvania Department of Education Classrooms for the Future (CFF) grant. When the state summarily cut this grant program after a few years, individuals districts were stuck with laptop upgrade bills. The CFF MacBook laptops received careful treatment from high school students, but the inevitable creeping gloom of technology obsolescence made the computers difficult to maintain. It was time to plan upgrades.

I shared with our school board a little chart that provoked a big discussion. Student-to-computer numbers for our three schools were approaching the 1:1 ratio. Marticville Middle School's ratio was 1.4 students for every computer. Penn Manor High School was at 2:1, not bad for a large high school. Four years of steady computer purchases brought us tantalizingly close to the point where every child would have a school computer. Data in hand, I asked the Penn Manor School Board of Directors "Is it time to consider a one-to-one device program?" To my surprise, the response was enthusiastic.

Of course, there were complications. Dr. Mike Leichliter, Penn Manor's Superintendent of Schools, and I explained how a one-to-one program would be a serious undertaking. Budgets mattered. Teacher professional development was vital. And there were support staff implications. It would not be a trivial project. The discussions ended with a plan to create an ad-hoc board committee charged with exploring the idea. Board member Johnna Friedman and I would co-chair the committee and return with a future recommendation. Johnna and I sought input from teachers and staff, but summer break was nearly upon us. The committee meetings would have to wait until autumn.

The summer of 2012 was hot and brisk. My team rolled out 1,000 laptops running Ubuntu 12.04 for district elementary schools. We launched our first Open Campus online courses. Shawn and Chad had several engineering projects cooking. The new Hambright Elementary School was under construction. It was yet another steamy summer in school IT land, and I was sweating the details of a one-to-one program.

School computing projects are complicated affairs. Making one happen takes leadership, meticulous planning, and thick skin. My IT Team is smaller than many districts of a similar size; supporting thousands of additional student devices would be a logistical challenge. Plus, I struggled with the toughest public school administrator question: What would it cost? Budgets are slim, technology staff resources are thin, and once you start a one-to-one program, you're in. Forever. I'm not aware of any schools that decided to take back the computers and replace them with calculators.

I had a hunch about the costs. We could probably afford to provide every child with a device if open source software was part of the equation. By shedding licensed software fees, we could purchase more computers for more students. The success of our elementary and middle school Linux programs proved that free and open source software worked and in no way limited the student learning experience.

However, cost savings would be pointless if we didn't think deeply about the learning objectives, and about our vision for what we wanted our students to do with personal computers. Technology is not inert. The nature of a gadget defines a student's learning options. If the committee decided to launch a digital reading program or reinforce rote skills via apps, a tablet would suffice. A bolder vision of learning would require devices with more sophisticated capabilities. However, to prevent my personal device biases from influencing the committee's decision, I planned to present tablets, Chromebooks, Mac, Linux, and Windows laptops for consideration. The committee would make the final device choice.

The Committee

The 16-person committee included classroom teachers from elementary through high school, as well as principals and district-level administrators. As the committee co-chair, my role was to facilitate conversations, listen, and learn from our teachers and staff. Any recommendation should be rooted in educational philosophy, not gadgets. I purposely excluded my technology staff from the committee meetings, which helped reinforce the primacy of learning. The device discussion would be the last point of the conversations.

Work commenced in November 2012. To start the discussion, I posed five guiding questions:

1. How would pervasive, consistent student access to technology support differentiated, cooperative learning?
2. Would the technology devices be a mere substitute for paper materials or a catalyst for higher-order critical thinking?
3. Would a one-to-one program support learning activities and projects that are not possible without consistent and immediate access to technology?
4. What support structures—professional development, technical, financial—would be required to implement and sustain a one-to-one program?
5. If we proceeded with a one-to-one program, where and when would we start? Which device would best support our vision of teaching and learning?

It didn't take long for the committee to agree that every student should carry a school computer. The group couldn't imagine a post-high school future where students would work without computers and Internet access. Staff and teachers couldn't accomplish their jobs without computing tools, and neither would our future graduates.

At the time, student access to laptops was limited. Without abundant classroom laptops, regular classroom technology integration wasn't happening. Shared laptop carts were particularly troublesome for middle and high school buildings. Twenty carts weren't enough to cover 120 classrooms.

And working with the laptops carts wasn't easy. Teachers had to sign out the cart (assuming one was available), retrieve the cart, push it to the classroom, unlock it, distribute the laptops to students, and note which student receives which machine. Next, the teachers would wrestle with problems like missing chargers or dead batteries. At the end of the class, they would package the whole bundle and push it down the hall to the next teacher. Fun times, indeed.

A one-to-one program would eliminate many of these time-sucking steps. But timely support was essential as well. Teachers would need help to get back on the rails when trouble arose. Gaps in tech support would lead to train wrecks. A massive influx of gear would strain my existing staff. The committee raised concerns about overtaxing our already stretched technology support team. The one-to-one program would require additional technology support staff. How would the school board respond to adding additional technology support positions?

A High School Focus

With quick agreement that the district should launch a one-to-one program, discussions turned to where to start. I kept my preconceptions from tainting the open decision-making process. Initially, I had thought the committee would recommend launching in grades seven and eight. The middle school student population was approximately half that of the high school. A middle school rollout would amount to a technology and professional development dress rehearsal before a huge high school one-to-one production. Plus, the middle schools could serve as the first purchase wave. Subsequent device purchases could flow into a full high school program over a period of two to three years.

Teachers nobly campaigned for their buildings and classrooms to go first. But as the committee reviewed the pros and cons for various grade levels, Penn Manor High School emerged as the obvious starting point.

Faculty readiness was the first factor. Penn Manor High School teachers were comfortable with technology integration thanks to the CFF grant. The CFF program provided extensive technology professional development workshops to help teachers make use of the new laptops. The CFF grant also provided funds for a dedicated, full-time technology professional development coach position. After the grant money had evaporated, Penn Manor High School continued to employ the technology coach position.

Given years of technology integration experience and the support of an embedded technology coach, the high school faculty pump was primed for a one-to-one program. The committee recognized high school teachers were best positioned to assimilate technology into their instructional design and classroom practices. The collective faculty resume included hands-on familiarity with project-based learning, differentiation of instruction, and an established tome of updated lesson plans built around student laptops. Plus, CFF project experiences helped high school teachers refine their technology grace under pressure. Teachers could keep rolling with a backup plan when a lesson was tripped up by laptop gremlins or network meltdowns. It takes true grit to stare down a class of headstrong seniors deprived of Wi-Fi.

A second decisive reason was the timing of the high school CFF device refresh cycle. Penn Manor High School received $471,000 to purchase 400 MacBook laptops and 14 carts in 2007. Students and teachers handled the CFF MacBooks with care. However, years of heavy use left the laptops dreaming of youthful days. As with most Apple products, planned obsolescence was not kind to the computers. Upgrades like new hard drives and RAM may have extended the system's usability for another year or two, but just like an old car that costs more to repair than replace, the laptops had reached the end of the road.

Fortunately, the school board and leadership team had the foresight to envision a day when the state CFF grant money well ran dry and every high school in Pennsylvania would be left holding the tab for a laptop upgrade. At the inception of the CFF program, the district established a designated capital reserve fund for future large-scale technology projects. The savings account contained enough cash to finance a post-CFF computer replacement cycle. If we were wise about what we purchased, the money could be stretched for a one-to-one program.

Network and wireless capacity was the third reason we decided to start with Penn Manor High School. Shortly after the high school CFF grant began, the district invested several hundred thousand dollars in upgrades to building network infrastructure and electrical capacity. During the facilities upgrade, my staff installed new Meru Networks 802.11n access points, which dramatically increased classroom wireless network coverage. Approximately 75 percent of the necessary wireless infrastructure was already in place. Expanding the wireless network to cover the gaps would require the addition of only a few access points and network switches.

The Open Campus virtual program was another reason for starting with high school students. New online courses were in development and Open Campus course enrollment was forecast to grow. The district provided a laptop to any student in need. Initially, most Open Campus students did not request a district laptop. However, demand for laptops would rise as additional students enrolled in future Open Campus courses.

Finally, high school technology needs were well defined. Math teachers were consistently using adaptive online math programs. Language Arts teachers had students blogging and podcasting. Science faculty made regular use of Logger Pro for experiments. Teachers across all departments incorporated Google Docs and Moodle into their instruction. Technology was not an afterthought—it was a natural part of teaching.

Every Device on the Table

The scene looked like a crew of high-class thugs robbed an electronics store and called an emergency business meeting to admire the loot. On the table in front of the committee were multiple laptops and tablets. Chromebooks, iPads, Android tablets, and laptops were spread out and ready to be poked and prodded by teachers and staff. It was time for the gadget talk. We had to select the one device for our one-to-one program.

Initial decisions came swiftly. High school faculty and staff agreed that a laptop would be the best option for students and teachers. The value of a full keyboard was too great to ignore. English and Language Arts teachers eloquently asserted that if the district was serious about writing skills, a keyboard was the most efficient writing instrument. The versatility of laptops, however, ruled the discussions. Students would benefit from the broad range of complex applications that were only available with a full computer. Students could construct podcasts, videos, digital media, and program in an environment designed to support deep learning through active engagement. The opportunities for students to create amazing work would be nearly limitless.

The committee dismissed both iPads and Android tablets. We could have added a keyboard for an added cost, but even so, tablets would not satisfy our student software needs. They would be great for consuming media, but teachers sought better tools for content creation. And Flash and Java—neither of which ran on iPad—were needed for many websites, especially simulation sites used by science teachers. On top of that, education-friendly programming software, such as Scratch, was not available on iPad. In fact, Apple rejected an early version of Scratch from the iPad App Store due to the company's policy of disallowing programs from running software code interpreters other than its own.[43]

Mac laptops were ruled out due to cost. The estimated price for 1,725 student Mac laptops was $1.7 million. Apple's laptop prices were too high. Given Apple's history of high prices, and with no cheaper Mac laptops available, the cost of an ongoing Mac laptop replacement cycle would be unsustainable as well.

The committee knew it could find suitable Windows laptops in the $400-$600 price range. Licensing for Microsoft Office, Windows, and other commercial software would inflate project costs. However, security was a concern as well. A fleet of 1,725 student Windows laptops would travel between the secured district network and dubious home wireless networks, coffee shops, and other potentially insecure access points. It is entirely possible to secure Windows operating systems, so long as one takes proper precautions. But managing Windows updates and security patches, at that scale, would require considerable attention from my team. The security challenge would be formidable.

Chromebooks, Not for Everyone

The committee's attention turned to the two most viable device candidates: the Google Chromebook and a PC laptop running Linux. Chromebooks, simplified laptops running Chrome OS, had emerged as low-cost Windows laptop alternatives. By 2013, educational momentum for Chromebooks was building as schools across the country replaced traditional Mac and Windows laptops with Google's web-centric laptops. It was easy to understand why. With models priced under $300, Chromebooks were an affordable option.

The committee reviewed several Chromebooks. All were lightweight, booted fast, and held a charge for an entire school day. The Chromebook checked many evaluation boxes. Moreover, my team would easily be able to support the devices via Google's web management dashboard. There was certainly a lot to like, but the disadvantages were troublesome.

Chromebooks are a victim of their simplicity. By trading away the native ability to install and run full local software programs, Chrome OS would not offer the range of sophisticated software necessary for Penn Manor High School students. Google Docs and Spreadsheets would be the only office-like options. The lack of Java was also a concern. Science teachers relied on educational programs and web simulations built with Java. Creating audio, video, and 3D projects with web apps would be possible on a Chromebook, but web apps were no match for dedicated open source applications like Audacity, Blender, KDEnlive, MuseScore, and OpenShot.

At the time, Chromebooks had limited offline options. Without Wi-Fi, many applications cease to function properly. Further, Chromebooks rely on just one web browser, Google Chrome. Alternative browsers like Firefox do not run on Chromebooks. Since educational websites can be slow to catch up to modern programming, the lack of browser choice might paint our students into a learning corner. And what would happen if future Department of Education testing software required a browser other than Chrome? With traditional laptops, students could easily switch browsers. Ultimately, the Chromebook was too narrow a device for our students.

The Linux Option

With the committee pruning the list of devices, I began suggesting that Linux running on PC laptops may be the win-win solution we needed. Linux provided all of the Chromebook capabilities and a lot more:

Rich educational software and computing capabilities—There would be few limits to what students could create with a Linux laptop. Thousands of programs were available for students to explore programming, 3D drawing, video, and audio. Locally installed software didn't require an Internet connection.

Multiple hardware choices—Linux runs on a wide array of PC hardware. With excellent portable laptops under $400, we would have plenty of options for screen size, shape, battery, processor, hard drive and RAM. Unlike tablets, students can connect the laptops to external devices via USB.

Secure and reliable—Linux security, reliability, and stability is legendary. At its core, it's designed to keep servers running for months or even years. Linux is also immune to Mac and Windows malware and viruses.

Technical Support—The successful elementary and middle school Linux program gave my team the experience and expertise needed to support desktop Linux. I had no doubts about providing support for a one-to-one Linux laptop program. If we needed outside assistance, the open source community would be a helpful resource.

Desktop Choices—Linux distributions support numerous unique desktop environments. We could customize the laptops to serve our needs. No other operating system offers the variety of desktop interfaces that Linux does.

State Testing Software Support—Pennsylvania's eDirect Classroom Diagnostic Tools and Keystone state exam software suite[44] run on Ubuntu Linux. The student laptops could support mandatory online state assessments.

Free Software—Apps, proprietary programs, and software subscriptions could have gobbled up the project budget, but Linux and open source software would reduce our software costs to near zero. The savings could be used to purchase more student devices, fund the next round of equipment purchases, or expand the program to additional grade levels. We could reinvest the savings into other school programs.

Free as in Freedom—Software released under the GPL and other open source licenses permits teachers and students to run, use, modify, learn from, improve upon, and share the software code. Even if a student chooses not to exercise these freedoms, open source licenses offer the potential, should a student decide to act upon it.

Big ideas—or ideals—are one thing, but our elementary school implementation proved that Linux was practical for classrooms. To help high school staff better understand Linux, I demoed a test laptop running Ubuntu, the distribution used in our elementary schools, as well as Ubermix, a special purpose distribution designed for education.[45] After spending time with demo laptops, the teachers agreed that both systems were suitable classroom options. And we all recognized that professional development would be needed no matter which operating system or device we selected.

Unlock the Laptop, Unlock Learning

During the demonstration of the Linux laptops, I suggested that we offer students unlocked administrative access (root) on their personal school device. A few people reacted like I threw a flaming Commodore 64 onto the conference table. Locking down school computers was an education tradition, like head lice checks and bad school lunches. For some, the notion of handing students the keys to their laptops was crazy talk. Students shouldn't install software or tinker with the operating system. Breaching student laptop security is taboo and subject to punishment by the school board.

Why is that? Public school technology policies often discourage experimentation. The school laptop is configured to run only the programs a teacher, principal, or technology director decrees acceptable. The practice infantilizes the student and removes agency from the learner. Without the ability to tune or modify their school computers, students are simply passengers on a programmer's, or principal's, virtual bus.

Think back to when you were young. Do you remember the playful joy of taking apart a favorite toy to discover how it worked or uncover what else it might do? Maybe you built Lego castles, tricked out your bicycle, or tinkered with the engine on your first car. It didn't matter that your first cardboard race car looked a little rough around the edges, or your first electronic experiment sparked like a Roman candle. By digging in, doing, deconstructing, and tinkering, humans experience intense and personal events that give rise to knowledge. Building and making, iteration and feedback—that's how we learn.

Dr. Seymour Papert, MIT mathematician, computer scientist, and educational computing visionary, summarized the relationship between students and computing in his seminal book Mindstorms: "In many schools today, the phrase 'computer-aided instruction' means making the computer teach the child. One might say the computer is being used to program the child. In my vision, the child programs the computer and, in doing so, both acquires a sense of mastery over a piece of the most modern and powerful technology and establishes an intimate contact with some of the deepest ideas from science, from mathematics, and from the art of intellectual model building."[46]

Schools, it seems, are holding computer policies upside down. They shackle incredible, open-ended learning technology in digital chains. An air of distrust hangs over the device and the student. The practice cripples learning and students' autonomy. Repressive computer device management policies crush learner agency and intellectual freedom.

Students should be trusted and respected. Their curiosity should be honored, and they should be enabled to create, explore, problem solve, and write. If we believe in these values, school policies need to change. If the vision is to trust kids and provide technology to amplify a student's potential, enable curiosity, and promote informal learning, then a school technology program should be appropriately open.

By providing students with unlocked laptops and the freedom to control their devices, we would be entering uncharted territory. But the committee agreed: Penn Manor students should be engineers and innovators, not technology tourists.

Trust in our students would be central to the one-to-one program. Students would receive local admin accounts, and with those "root accounts," have full and unrestricted permission to explore and examine the Linux operating system. They would have freedom to spin software configuration knobs and personalize their desktops. They could freely install and experiment with a universe of open source programs. And, of course, a few students would stampede like wild bulls in a china shop and create software chaos on their computers. But those raging bulls just might be future innovators in the making. Their passion should be encouraged, not corralled.

Principles, Values, and Vision

By March 2013, the committee was in full agreement to recommend a one-to-one laptop program running Linux and open source software at Penn Manor High School during the 2013-2014 school year. The last step was for me to synthesize the committee's voice and write our philosophy and values. I drafted a mission statement and six guiding principles drawn from the discourse. At the next school board meeting, I would present the committee recommendation, vision, and six guiding principles:

Our vision is that all students will use technology to energize personal intellectual development and construct knowledge for college, careers, and beyond.

Anytime, Anyplace Learning—Personal laptops will be a student's travel companion for his or her entire academic career. Importantly, anytime/anyplace means the lines between school learning and home learning are abolished. With technology access barriers removed, students may work at a time and place of their choosing. Impromptu home learning opportunities are now possible as education moves beyond the walls of a traditional school building.

Curiosity and Agency—We wish to incite students to direct and take ownership of their learning. Their curiosity should not be confined to the classroom or bound by a locked technology device. Students are encouraged to tinker with the laptops, spin software knobs, and delve into a powerful set of learning software and creative programs. Exploration and discovery is a key goal of the one-to-one computing initiative. Students are trusted and given administrative access to their computers. They may install software, explore the operating system, code, or even run a local web server.

Equity of Access—Equal access to a flexible and potent computer provides learning opportunities for students who may not otherwise have access to current technology. In contrast to traditional computer-on-a-cart models, where technology intermittently visits a classroom for a special learning occasion, the laptops will be a permanent instructional companion, both in school and at home. Personal device ownership heralds a seismic shift in student learning opportunities. Classroom ecologies will change as we meet students on their own technology-rich playing field and then ask them to up their game. All students, regardless of socio-economic status, will be equal players in a new school ethos.

Engagement and Ownership—Research indicates that one-to-one programs have considerable positive impact on student motivation. Schools report a decline in discipline issues and measurable increase in student engagement. When we trust our students to take ownership of a personal, customizable, potent, and dynamic learning tool, we believe our school culture will fundamentally change as well.

Science Technology Engineering and Math—Laptops are computational and analytical devices for engineering, math, and science. By offering the inherent flexibility of a full laptop, students will develop problem-solving abilities and practice higher-order thinking. These skills are now, more than ever, essential to empowering our students for the new economy and ultra-globalized workforce.

Writing and Language Arts—The flat-world technology revolution asks us to rethink our notion of what it means to be educated and literate in the 21st Century. However, one traditional skill remains unchanged: the ability to artfully and effectively self-express through writing. Blogs, reports, essays, and Tweets; writing across multiple modalities is learning made visual–and a full keyboard is still the most efficient tool to hone this skill.

For school leadership readers, I must emphasize how important it is to define your goals and values before launching any large-scale technology program. A clear vision of your program's purpose is essential. The Penn Manor one-to-one program guiding principles served as a strategic lens to focus our instructional, operational, and fiscal planning. Today, the principles and values continue to guide school board and administrative discussions. I expect the guiding principles will inform our planning efforts for years to come.

The School Board Plan

On April 1, 2013, after two separate public presentations and discussions, the Penn Manor Board of School Directors unanimously voted for the committee's recommendation to launch a one-to-one laptop program at Penn Manor High School. The program was scheduled to start in four months. Approximately 100 students enrolled in Open Campus online courses would form a pilot laptop group starting in September 2013. A full-building implementation for all students in grades 9 through 12 would begin in January 2014. Students would receive a laptop to use during the school day and to take home on evenings and weekends.

Dr. Philip Gale, the high school principal, conceived the idea of a fall pilot, followed by a launch in the second semester. Penn Manor follows a block schedule, with four student courses scheduled during each of its two semesters. The second semester begins in January each year and is akin to the start of a new school year. By waiting until mid-year to launch the full program, there would be sufficient time to gather feedback from the pilot, refine the technology, provide teacher professional development, and engage with parents. The project plan components included:

Professional Development—Faculty professional development would be essential to achieving the one-to-one program goals and vision. Teachers and students would receive many new open source software programs. We planned for three days of teacher technology training throughout the school year. There was a lot the disciplines and departments could learn from and share with each other.

Policy Development—The laptops would travel home with students, and we needed to create one-to-one laptop agreement and policy documents before the September 2013 pilot began. Dr. Leichliter and I would work with school board members and our attorneys to create the policy by July 2013.

Infrastructure and Operations—District Internet connectivity was 100Mbs. Using past usage trends, I calculated we would have sufficient bandwidth during the first year, but we needed to plan for additional capacity in the next 24 months. Increased Internet connectivity would serve the high school and provide capacity for the one-to-one program's possible expansion into the middle schools. Internal wireless was mostly robust and reliable. The high school building was well-covered with wireless, but a few weak spots remained. We would fill in the dead spots during the summer and upgrade network switch capacity as needed.

Parent Communication—Principal Gale would write letters to parents announcing the program. He and I would conduct parent workshops to address questions and concerns during fall 2013. I would create a parent FAQ document to address common questions about the devices and the program.[47]

Laptop Selection—The committee recommended a PC laptop running Linux, but we hadn't decided which laptop. My team and I would review models during the spring and make a decision in early summer. Students would test the laptops during the fall 2013 program pilot. We would select a laptop and case by the end of October 2013.

Damage and Insurance—Public schools commonly charge a technology fee to cover the use of a device and potential damage. However, the administrative team was not comfortable forcing insurance fees that many never use. Parents and students would not be asked to pay an annual insurance or technology fee. The solution was to implement a "you break it, you bought it" policy: the district asked students and parents to pay for damage or loss of the laptop, both on and off school grounds. Students who did not agree to be responsible for damage outside of school could keep their laptops at school during the evenings and weekends.

Software—Student laptops would run a Linux distribution and open source software exclusively. Linux would provide students with professional computing software, as well as the ability to control and customize their laptops. My team would augment the base Linux installation with standard software programs. To comply with the U.S. Federal Children's Internet Protection Act (CIPA) and prevent access to pornographic websites, the laptops would use the district's web content filter inside the school network and at home.

Student Help Desk—Timely and helpful support would be essential to the laptop program. We planned to create an elective course composed of Penn Manor High School student technology apprentices. However, one additional technology staff member was needed. The new position would help existing staff focus on the one-to-one program.

Student Freedom and Trust—Penn Manor will trust students. Students would have root account access to the school laptop. They would be permitted—in fact, encouraged—to install programs, tinker with laptop settings, and experiment with software as they learn the art and science of computing.

Cost Estimates—Pairing a low-cost device with free and open source software enabled us to afford a laptop for every student in grades 9 through 12. The estimated cost for the entire high school—1,725 students—was $578,000. That money would come from the district capital reserve fund.

Without the advocacy and trust of our school board, the one-to-one program would have probably resembled a traditional closed-technology project. Open source software, student root access, and our student team added a unique twist to the program. Providing root access to students provoked a few dramatic responses. Ken Long, Penn Manor Board President, was openly candid with his (legitimate) concern for student and teacher security and safety, saying, "It scares the hell out me." However, Long and other school board members trusted my team and me. I described how the student wireless network was separate from the staff network and how Linux is immune to Windows viruses. When board members learned more about open source software and understood how each student would have independent access to their personal laptop, they grew confident my team could balance open technology learning opportunities with security.

Student Staffing Solutions

At its April 1, 2013, meeting, the Penn Manor School Board voted to create a new data specialist position. The position, currently held by Dianne Bates, would take over the day-to-day work of coordinating student data collection and reporting for the Pennsylvania Department of Education (PDE) and oversee the district student information system. PDE's intricate school data system was onerous; we needed dedicated staff to keep the district in compliance with mandatory reports. I planned to shift data responsibilities away from me, our help desk specialist Gina Kostelich and, to some extent, building technical staff. With data duties assigned to a new individual, I could position my team to support the one-to-one program and Student Help Desk.

However, another problem remained. In 2012, Penn Manor's IT staff per student ratio was in the bottom third of districts in our region. My small team had always delivered big results with few resources, but the scale of this project was different. I had to keep Alex Lagunas from dreaming of legions of monster machines chasing him in the night. Alex is an outstanding technologist. His excellent problem-solving skills and hardy work ethic are legendary. Nevertheless, the mass-influx of laptops, on top of caring for hundreds of existing high school staff devices, would stretch him thin.

Alex welcomed the challenge, but we'd need more hands. And we both knew the solution was not more adult staff. The best solution would be our students.

A close-knit team of four high school students spent the past few summers volunteering with the Penn Manor IT Department. Rather than enjoy their vacation time, the student crew assisted my staff with summer IT maintenance and computer updates. As the technical prowess of those students grew, Alex and I challenged them with increasingly intricate technical projects. We'd known the students for years, and they had proven dependable and highly capable of assisting with the day-to-day technical needs of our high school.

In the fall of 2012, two of the students, Andrew Lobos and Benjamin Thomas, worked with my team and Penn Manor High School staff to create a sophisticated Career Day event registration and scheduling system. Two other students, Nick Joniec and Collin Enders, were long-standing summer IT volunteers. The quartet was ecstatic about the idea of providing one-to-one peer technical support during their upcoming senior year.

A student-led technology support program would be new to Penn Manor High School. However, Principal Gale embraced the progressive vision and enthusiastically backed a plan to expand the independent study course into a full help desk experience. We would entrust the students to work as apprentices alongside the IT staff and me during the school day.

The technology plan was in place. Open source software would power the laptops. But open source culture would carry our classrooms further. In the next chapter, we'll meet the remarkable student apprentices who helped build our one-to-one laptop program and open source school technology community.

6
Student Apprentices

Close your eyes and think back to your high school days. A teacher stands at the front of a stuffy square room. He lectures, drawing with gritty chalk, while a murmur of facts, figures, and dates pours from his mouth into a grid of neatly arranged desks. He rambles. Students apathetically scrawl notes—words and numbers in transit toward regurgitation during an exam. He expects every student to master precisely the same information, no matter their individual ability, personal strengths, interests, or aptitudes. A bell chimes, and students sleepwalk to the next lecture where the cycle repeats itself. Lecture, worksheet, test, repeat. Students endure and count the days for four years. Those who make it receive a rectangular paper reward memorializing a well-played academic game. The ordeal ends, and a life nothing like a high school classroom commences.

The Internet changed learning. It ate the traditional lecture-and-test school model alive, and danced on its bones. Memorization and recall doesn't count for much when the world's information is a Google search away. Equipped with a laptop and web browser, students can learn anything they need, in any order, at any time, from any expert with a YouTube video or course website. As someone said, any teacher who can be replaced by YouTube should be.

The lifeless lecture meme persists in our culture. Every time I hear adults remark "That's the way school was for us, why change?", I want to throw a World Book Encyclopedia against a wall (if I could find one). Our culture still clings to the notion that great teachers orally transmit sacrosanct curriculum into kids' heads by the power of cunning lecture charm and wit. Although few people have the charisma to deliver riveting lecture monologues, mass-downloading data into student brains is still accepted as a common instructional strategy in many schools.

Before the Internet, we had an equally inert metaphor for classroom lectures: banking deposits. In his book, Pedagogy of the Oppressed, educator and philosopher Paulo Freire likens lectures to information deposits made into a banking account:

"Narration (with the teacher as narrator) leads the students to memorize mechanically the narrated account. Worse yet, it turns them into 'containers,' into 'receptacles' to be 'filled' by the teachers. The more completely she fills the receptacles, the better a teacher she is. The more meekly the receptacles permit themselves to be filled, the better students they are.

Education thus becomes an act of depositing, in which the students are the depositories and the teacher is the depositor. Instead of communicating, the teacher issues communiques and makes deposits which the students patiently receive, memorize, and repeat. This is the 'banking' concept of education, in which the scope of action allowed to the students extends only as far as receiving, filing, and storing the deposits."[48]

Freire suggests the banking model is an instrument of intellectual oppression. As a student succumbs to the teacher's absolute view of world knowledge, the teacher-learner relationship becomes one of compliance and domination.

"It follows logically from the banking notion of consciousness that the educator's role is to regulate the way the world 'enters into' the students. The teacher's task is to organize a process which already occurs spontaneously, to 'fill' the students by making deposits of information which he or she considers to constitute true knowledge...Verbalistic lessons, reading requirements, the methods for evaluating 'knowledge,' the distance between the teacher and the taught, the criteria for promotion: everything in this ready-to-wear approach serves to obviate thinking."[49]

Writing in 1970, Freire accurately predicted the future of school. Today's closed education models define success by the content a student has purportedly mastered, as demonstrated by test scores, along a linear learning route. Knowledge unveils, one lesson at a time, as students load up on facts from commissioned "tourist-stops." Algebra appears before Calculus; World War 1 before World War 2; Biology before Chemistry before Physics. Students who capitulate, mark the correct worksheet answers, and stay on the course receive the top institutional prize: a 4.0 (or higher) GPA.

Step off the school tour bus, and the music abruptly shifts from a military march to free jazz. Beyond the closed schoolhouse, there's no grading scale or curriculum scope and sequence. Learning is all Ornette Coleman and Stravinsky. We learn from poking the world around us and jumping as the world pokes back in delightfully unusual ways. We learn from stumbling into side alleyways of failure, bad hunches, and fortuitous flubs. Learning is interactive, unexpected, and chaotic. Knowledge comes from getting kicked to the curb, from nailing the high C note, and from improvising on the fly. Learning how to learn is the killer skill for the street-wise student.

What if our classrooms pushed aside lecture and standard curriculum, and reorganized as a community of practitioners working toward a common goal? What if every high school junior worked just like a journalist or technologist? The Penn Points student journalism course proved students can soar when they are trusted as equal partners in a meaningful project and invested in the program's success or failure. Why not apply the same collaborative model to a student technology help desk?

I knew we would be exploring new territory with unfamiliar theme music. Linux and open source software rarely make an appearance in schools, let alone on laptops poised to accompany students between their classrooms and homes. Standardized curriculum doesn't help when one breaks new ground. However, this would be the ultimate problem-based technology learning opportunity for high school student apprentices. What would happen if they played a key role in their classmates' success? Given agency, opportunity, and trust, could they construct a technology community for their peers?

Assembled around a common purpose, unchained from a scripted curriculum, and given the freedom to learn based on personal interests and passions, our students rose to the occasion in unique and wonderful ways.

Andrew and Nick

Today's students turn to apps or the web to find out if school is canceled due to inclement weather. Not Andrew; he built a robot.

As Andrew Lobos passionately described his new school closure alert robot, it was obvious he wasn't a typical seventh-grade student. The PHP[50] program he wrote vigilantly monitored the district website for announcements. The script checked in every five minutes and evaluated the section of the district's HTML page that displayed emergency notifications. If the school-closing news appeared, his program signaled an Arduino[51] micro-controller, which commanded a little robot servo dial to rotate an arrow towards a cardboard sign inscribed with the word

"Closed." If Andrew awoke to the arrow still pointing to the cardboard "Open" sign, it was time to catch the bus.

Precocious isn't a strong enough word to describe Andrew. His problem-solving gifts were extraordinary, and his love of technology was infectious. Andrew first used Linux in the fifth grade to build a web server on an old Pentium III computer he found in his parent's basement. By the age of 13, he maintained a website, Andrew's Tech Show, to host code for his robotics projects. At the end of seventh grade, he researched and recommended to me, in a detailed five bullet point email, a plan for upgrading the middle school TV studio equipment and production workflows. He was the undisputed robotics and software programming expert in the Technology Student Association (TSA) club.[52] As he talked about his home server setup or his latest programming experiment, I could close my eyes and almost forget I wasn't chatting with a member of my IT staff.

At the close of the school year, as the rest of his classmates watched the obligatory last-week-of-school class movies, Andrew emailed me asking to assist the tech team with computer support around the building. When he inquired about summer technology intern opportunities, I jumped at the chance to have him work with my staff on summer computer maintenance. By his eighth-grade year, I arranged for Andrew to slip out of his middle school activity periods—and sometimes regular classes—to provide laptop tutoring for Assistant Superintendent Ellen Pollock and Elementary Coordinator Vickie Hallock.

Ellen later recalled: "Andrew, whose middle school was attached to the district office, would quietly appear in my office doorway several times a week during his activity period. He would have already consulted with Charlie about the content of my session for that day and we would spend a half hour or so together. 'Let's practice working with the trackpad instead of the mouse.' 'Let's do some bookmarking.' 'Today we're going to learn to Skype with one of the elementary classrooms.' 'For next time, practice these three things…'

"His tremendous value to me, as an adult, was that he could instruct at a level well below his sophisticated knowledge of technology without making me feel silly or stupid when I asked a question or worked through a procedure. Even as an eighth-grader, he had a maturity and respect for individuals and their varying technology abilities way beyond his years. In this, he was able to mimic, without even being aware of this gift, the instructional techniques I so valued in our district technology staff, so much so that I hired him to work with my 80-year-old mother at her home on basic computer skills. Of course, he was in eighth grade at the time and didn't drive, so my mother or I would pick him up and take him home."

In the spring of 2010, before moving on to Penn Manor High School, Andrew worked with teaching staff to create a schedule sorting program for Manor Middle School's Sports Day. Fellow students would sign up for various activities via a Google Form which added their selections to a Google spreadsheet. His software ingested the spreadsheet data and automatically sorted requests into a field day event schedule. The programming was stunning for a 14-year-old. Furthermore, it would become the kernel of a much more sophisticated scheduling program ultimately used for Career Day seminar registration at Penn Manor High School.

...

Nick Joniec was a high school freshman with a business card and client reference list. After his school shift ended, Nick was busy building a freelance computer consulting business. His website advertised in-home training, computer repair, and network help. He was earning money as a home computer guru and trainer for clients in his neighborhood, including one of his former middle school teachers. The 15-year-old balanced technology house calls and homework while getting straight A's in all of his classes.

Teacher Susan Baldrige introduced me to Nick, who was a student in the Penn Points journalism class. Nick was a capable writer, but Susan recognized his technical talent and suggested we interview him for the Penn Points webmaster role. Five minutes into the conversation, I could tell he was incredibly smart, but I also sensed maturity and poise well beyond his age. Nick was mature and polite; he conveyed life experience acquired by supporting adult clients. He was a 30-something young professional, temporarily masquerading as a high school freshman.

Driven and talented, Nick was a natural born student leader. And like Andrew, he was a gifted communicator. His emails to technology staff and me were always courteous and articulate—a refreshing departure from the informal missives one typically receives from students.

Andrew and Nick spent several weeks interning with my IT staff the summer before their sophomore year. Close friends since third grade at Eshleman Elementary School, their talents differed but complemented one another. Nick was a self-described "hardware guy" who loved taking apart computers and getting down and gritty with cables, drives, and cases. But he was also a natural coordinator and manager, and would take the lead on the projects we assigned to the duo. Andrew excelled at software and programming. He was content to work behind the screens on tasks like operating system configuration and system imaging, the process of cloning a standard master software bundle to hundreds or even thousands of computers. Together, they formed a dependable and productive team unlike any I'd known since we began including students in technology projects like the 2001 custom PC build.

By the start of the 2011 summer vacation break, the trustworthy and tenacious duo was eager to tackle any technology challenge we threw at them. Alex Lagunas assigned them much more intricate work than moving, unboxing, and repairing computers. Under his guidance, the two apprentices took on rebuilding software images for the high school computer labs. They also helped with troubleshooting faculty and staff technical issues.

Both apprentices would ultimately become core partners in the one-to-one program launch, but their summer volunteer work was equally notable. By the time they graduated in June 2014, Andrew and Nick had clocked over 450 summer internship hours—more than any past Penn Manor student. How many teenagers would give up nearly all of their summer vacation to work in a miserably hot high school simply because they loved learning?

Students Sort It Out

Andrew and Nick were eager for new challenges in their junior year. With open schedule slots for elective courses, they opted for an independent study programming course. The duo used the time to learn programming languages and to build web applications. Andrew had several projects on his learning list, including a complete rewrite of his middle school Sports Day scheduling software. Penn Manor High School staff heard about his middle school program and were eager to adopt something similar for the High School Career Day seminar selection and scheduling process.

Penn Manor High School's Career Day was an annual event where dozens of professionals presented mini-seminars on their jobs and workplace. Students could select up to three workshops from a roster of nearly 70 sessions from professionals such as bankers, EMTs, graphic designers, engineers, and business owners. The program was a fun way for students to explore careers. However, the paper and spreadsheet scheduling process created pain and suffering for guidance counselors. They would spend days sorting and sifting 1,700 students into workshops, all the while trying to balance student choices with room seating and speaker availability. Special cases, such as scheduling all ninth-graders into an assembly during one of the three morning sessions, made the scheduling exercise wholly convoluted. They were thrilled that Andrew would help ease the pain.

To get the project started, I took Andrew to a design and development meeting with guidance office staff. Together we reviewed what was needed to gather and process the event registrations. Students would go to a web page, enter their name, and select up to four speaker sessions. The Career Day software would need administrative screens to create those sessions, define topic categories, and set maximum room-seating capacities. The control panel screen would need options to start the sort and add new students to session rosters. The final step, after students were successfully scheduled, would be to create a PDF of rosters and an attendance list for the speakers.

The sorting algorithm had to fulfill every student's first and second session choice despite several tricky constraints. Three separate sessions ran on Career Day: two for students to attend guest speaker talks and one for a mandatory assembly. The program would need to juggle up to four student career session choices, and the final schedule had to include the assembly. Upper classmen selections received priority.

If the software couldn't successfully satisfy a student's requests, the algorithm attempted to fill the schedule with an alternate session from the same category group. For example, say a student was interested in the EMT workshop, but seating was full. She would be redirected into a family doctor session. Failing that, the sorting algorithm would attempt to fill her schedule with any randomly open session. It was quite a puzzle.

Andrew worked diligently from the high school technology office every day during fourth block. By early October 2012, he'd reshaped his original middle school sorting program, updating the code to satisfy the new Career Day sign-up and scheduling system requirements. He created the web portal, sorting algorithm, and database using PHP and MySQL, two open source software tools. For a junior student, it was a dense project with a knotty sorting problem.

Andrew coordinated with me, Alex, and Chad Billman, but the work was entirely his own. My team and I contributed only guidance and advice. Frankly, the 16-year-old programmer didn't need much technical help. His skills were exemplary. However, I later discovered Andrew had a friend working, and learning, alongside him to code the software's student and teacher screens. He sent me an email containing a link to the beta version of the Career Day program—running on his home development server, of course. The very last line of his message revealed his mysterious partner: "Also, I think I mentioned to you that I would like to use this as a group project for the TSA competition. The HTML, CSS and JavaScript for the signup was done by Ben Thomas (cc'd on this email)."

Ben

I'm not certain if Ben Thomas was wearing his GitHub[53] shirt the very first time we met, but I have a hard time picturing him without it. While classmates walked about in T-shirts emblazoned with images of favorite rock bands or sports idols, Ben's shirt advertised the open source community's most popular destination for sharing code.

I later discovered Andrew and Ben were friends and fellow robotics enthusiasts. The Career Day program wasn't their first technical collaboration. As members of LANLords, one of Lancaster County's FIRST[54] robotics teams, they had competed in several competitive robotics events. Along with Nick, they participated in the Penn Manor TSA Club and had designed electronics projects for regional and state competitions.

Andrew regarded graphics and user interfaces as "the bane of his existence." He enlisted his friend Ben to craft the front-end website designs and visual styles, which gave Andrew more time to focus on fine-tuning the underlying sorting algorithm and scheduling engine. For Ben, the timing was perfect. He was teaching himself Bootstrap,[55] a popular open source HTML/CSS code framework for web interfaces created by developers at Twitter.

Ben later told me, "I got really into styling our TSA team website. We used Bootstrap at that point, but when we wrote the Career Day Program, we didn't use Bootstrap. I looked at how Bootstrap worked and figured out containing systems and other components, and we wrote custom styles for the program's buttons and graphics. I learned how to make a user interface designed for students that would be easy to use. It was just something I was interested in, and I think it turned out nicely."

To make coordinating their efforts easier, Andrew and Ben used GitHub to store code, track their progress, and review each other's work. They learned from YouTube and online code examples. Without a course rubric, curriculum, or end-of-unit test, they created software destined to impact 1,725 of their peers, and eliminate hundreds of staff hours typically wasted on manually sorting and scheduling students into sessions.

On November 29, 2012, Andrew, Ben, and I met with high school guidance office staff to demo the nearly complete Career Day program. Guidance staff were excited. It was soon time to go live.

I trusted Andrew and Ben, and I was comfortable the system was ready for hundreds of high school students to poke and prod. My team reviewed and tested the software. However, I couldn't help but fear a failure would be a spectacular blow to the student programmers, and to the idea of enlisting students to build real production software. But Andrew was poised and on point. "There was no pressure. I was confident I could make it work," he said.

Penn Manor High School's Career Day website went live in January 2013. Incidentally, this was about two months before the one-to-one committee made its program recommendation to the school board. Andrew and Ben's program performed flawlessly. Students signed up for sessions without any problems. Once everyone made their selections, the algorithm shuffled and sorted more than 1,700 picks into near perfect schedules in about 500 milliseconds. Guidance staff was jubilant. Andrew and Ben just saved them days of sorting. Marjean Long, the Career Day event coordinator, expressed her enthusiasm:

"The process went so smoothly for the students when they made their session choices; it was so efficient that the program did everything that we wanted it to and it produced rapid results! In the past, I had to hand-count all of the student requests for speakers and sort them so that the rooms were not overflowing, then tally up who did sign up by going through paper lists of student rosters. The program gave me days and days of work time back!"

Andrew, who had already developed a reputation as a programming whiz, had put another feather in his coding cap. But for Ben, the mystery student who emerged out of nowhere, the moment was an inflection point in his high school career. Suddenly, he was a rising and recognized student star. His success helped him focus on academics. Between his freshman and senior years, he progressed from career prep courses, to college prep, to honors level courses, including Honors Calculus. After Ben completed his college freshman year, he told me: "I didn't really connect with school; what they were teaching me didn't have any effect. I had other interests like robotics and technology. But I realized if I wanted to make a career out of this, I had to step up my game and focus in class."

Ben was finding his passion, and it was marvelous to watch him flourish. I don't know that he could have found his voice through a traditional curriculum. Given trust and the opportunity to build a personally meaningful and authentic program, Ben achieved a success that no high-stakes standardized test could measure. He created software for every one of his classmates. "It was awesome being able to design something, and have it be appreciated...and the counseling department loved me after that!" he said.

A month later, Andrew and Ben beamed with pride as they demonstrated the Career Day sign-up and sorting system at the Pennsylvania Educational Technology Conference and Expo Student Showcase on February 12, 2013. As they chatted about their software tools and techniques with visiting teachers and school educational technology staff, it was apparent their work was more advanced than anything else in the high school student showcase. The Career Day program could have passed as a college-level programming project.

As I sat with them at lunch that day, I knew unequivocally that the Penn Manor one-to-one program had to have a student-led technology help desk. These amazing young hackers would be part of the perfect open team.

The First Student Help Desk

By August 2013, Penn Manor's official Student Help Desk program was online. Dr. Philip Gale designated it an honors-level independent study course. There were no course prerequisites—everyone with the curiosity and desire to learn was welcome. There was no formal curriculum. Students would learn alongside my team, and together we would figure out what we needed when we needed it. There were no exams; this was a results-only learning environment, not an academic exercise.

Five seniors represented the core help desk. Andrew Lobos, Ben Thomas, and Nick Joniec were there, as well as their mutual friend, Collin Enders. Collin had interned with my team for the previous two summers and he possessed extensive technology experience via TSA and FIRST robotics. He and his three friends formed the nucleus of the inaugural help desk team and served as mentors to incoming students new to technology support. Benjamin Moore, a student with little IT background beyond the motivation to learn more about computers, was the fifth apprentice. Ben Moore's first love was theater production, but he decided on a whim that the Student Help Desk would be interesting. He thought computers were cool and wanted to learn to code.

Between the five students' schedules, I had help desk coverage from the start of school until the ending bell. Apprentices reported to the help desk room just like they would to any other course on their schedule. All similarity to a traditional math or science class ended once they entered the room. The help desk was a serious operation, and our first deadline was looming. In less than two weeks, a pilot group of 90 high school students would receive laptops. We needed the apprentices to help us prepare for the pilot program, and for the full one-to-one program launch in January 2014.

The help desk classroom, Room 358, was just off the high school library, a place once reserved for the Penn Points student newsroom. I couldn't ignore the single Penn Points Staff T-shirt still fastened to the far wall. It was a fitting reminder of the remarkable collaborative work that began in that room. Now the space was crowded with a wagonload of sinuous network cables, power adapters, carry cases, mice, USB drives, and towers of boxes filled with demo laptops waiting patiently for the chance to greet their new student owners.

To better supervise the students' activities, Alex relocated his desk from the high school technology office to the Student Help Desk room. With no physical separation between the student and the staff spaces, the apprentices couldn't evade oversight. But Alex wasn't there to bark orders to minions. His role was that of a team leader and co-worker. He directed day-to-day support activities, and mentored the young team on everything from repairs to programming tricks. Together, as teacher and apprentice, the entire affair resembled an 18th-century French atelier—except with less painting, and more programming.

It would soon become difficult to discern the line between staff technician and student apprentice. Support roles overlapped and visitors received equal assistance from the apprentices and IT staff. As this community evolved, the student apprentices became even more passionate and energetic. They loved the work and felt a deep commitment to the mission and purpose of the laptop project. As the weeks progressed, any lingering fears that students couldn't make this happen quickly evaporated.

The student team was tight-knit, and remarkably good at self-organizing. Each student apprentice found an individual role. Collin and Nick were quick to tackle logistics and organizational tasks. Andrew and Ben Thomas preferred writing code. And the core quartet took it upon themselves to welcome and help Ben Moore.

Project-based learning? Check. Everything the student apprentices created was part of an authentic technology project. Challenge-based learning? Absolutely. We had four months to do something the high school has never done. How about 20 percent time? Certainly. Innovation was encouraged 100 percent of the time. Hour of code? Plural. Our apprentices were about to log hundreds of hours of programming time.

We had created a paradise for student hackers.

Hackers Will Not Be Expelled

In the first few minutes of the 1985 movie "The Breakfast Club," you may notice a brief still shot of an old-school computer lab. Hanging on the wall, above the relic IBM terminals, is a blunt sign reading "Hackers Will Be Expelled." In most schools, times haven't changed much since then. At Penn Manor High School, the joyful love of hacking permeated the early help desk. Hacking was not a concept or skill we taught. It was an ethos we embraced. Our role was to clear obstacles, provide prompts, and create a culture where trial and risk receive encouragement and praise.

Spontaneous projects sprouted from the bubbling mud of creativity and purpose. Midway through the laptop pilot semester, I was stunned by a new addition to the help desk room. A massive, full-color vinyl banner advertised the Student Help Desk. Draped like a coat of arms across the classroom's largest whiteboard, the prodigious size of the sprawling banner momentarily took me aback. The student team gleefully announced Nick had worked with his dad, in their home garage, to create the sign. It was glorious.

A sense of purpose also promoted engagement and innovation. Nick later took it upon himself to design and print ID badges for the team. He crafted a lovely badge; the design was polished and professional. But the student team didn't settle with an ID badge. Ben Thomas saw an opportunity to play with his newly acquired USB RFID[56] card reader and stepped in to improve the identification system. Why stop with an ID badge when they could have an integrated sign-in system? He added a RFID button to the ID badge. When each apprentice arrived at the beginning of class, they waved the badge at Ben's RFID reader and clocked in.

The RFID reader was attached to a Raspberry Pi computer, and a program watched for sign-in events. His software passed the RFID check-in, and the ID of the student apprentice, to the student ticket support program he and Andrew had created. The support software then displayed a page showing which apprentices were currently available to offer assistance. Since the support page was public, students and teachers could check to see if an apprentice was on-duty before trekking across the high school to reach the help desk room.

The student apprentices created three important software programs. The first was the Fast Linux Deployment Toolkit (FLDT). FLDT is a software mass-imaging system Andrew created after he and fellow apprentices grew frustrated by limitations with a program called FOG. The second project was a student laptop and inventory tracking and ticket system built by Andrew and Ben. The third, a URL-sharing program called PaperPlane, was born from a staff idea that turned into a student challenge. You'll learn more about these three programs in the next chapter.

Other projects were less practical and much more playful. Collin's favorite funny memory about the help desk was a mischievous prank—"trolling" Ben. "I worked with Andrew to secretly install a program on his laptop. Once every hour, a Cron job triggered the machine to speak out loud the phrase 'I'm watching you!' He had no idea what was going on. That was fun to watch."

Thinking about Ben Thomas' laptop inexplicably blurting "I'm watching you!" in the middle of a quiet class still makes me break from the role of serious school official and laugh out loud like a schoolboy. The whimsical caper invokes the genuine spirit of hacking and reminds me that schools shouldn't be glum factories of curriculum and testing. When you let students go, when you trust them, you change their world.

Students as Teachers

Moving away from old, familiar software can be daunting for teachers with limited time and mountains of grading. Software upgrades are fun for programmers but nerve-wracking for educators who just want to get on with teaching. Training and tech support are essential, but they're often in short supply. When I told Christa Craig, Penn Manor Business Technologies teacher, our last high school computer labs would disappear when we moved to one-to-one student laptops, she was nervous and stressed.

For many years, Christa's department taught accounting basics with a textbook series called Automated Accounting. The text included companion software initially written for Windows XP and 2000. My team had a terrible time making the Neolithic software run on Windows 7, let alone any other operating systems. With the one-to-one program launching in three months, it was time to upgrade. Alex and I recommended an open source program called GnuCash.[57] The software is similar to the commercial Quicken program, and includes features for small business accounting.

Christa began experimenting with GnuCash and felt that it had the features she needed to teach the principles of double-entry bookkeeping. Time to master a new program was in short supply, so we found a better solution: help from technology apprentice Nick Joniec. She emailed me one morning in November 2013: "Nick is teaching my Accounting I class how to use GnuCash, and is doing an awesome job!!!"

She later recounted the experience with Nick during a May 2015 interview with Red Hat Films:

"When Nick said that he understood the program, and he could help with it, it felt a little strange at first. Nick was a great asset to my accounting class because he was able to explain the program to me a little bit better. And the two of us worked together to be able to teach the other students how to do it. He said, 'Hey, Mrs. Craig, we can do this together.' And it worked out well."

Trusting students as co-facilitators—what better way is there to building deep engagement than through the experience of teaching a topic to one's peers? But in practice, this takes courage and vision to trust students as collaborators. Christa continues:

"It was a new experience collaborating with a student on teaching. It wasn't so much that he was instructing me how to do it. He was just explaining what he knew and helping me learn from him. He felt valuable in the class, as well."

Open-minded teachers like Christa gave our apprentices an opportunity to build self-esteem and leadership skills that would transfer to a myriad of careers, whether related to technology or not. Most compelling, I think, is that a whole new school culture emerged. The roles of student and teacher blurred. The classroom hierarchy flattened. We were becoming an open schoolhouse.

7
Building the One-to-One Program

It was August 2013. My team was in for a challenge. We had less than five months to scale from a one-to-one laptop pilot project of 90 students to a full implementation for the entire high school. The program was scheduled to launch by the end of January 2014, just as the second semester was about to start. There were many moving parts: community and parent engagement, teacher professional development, software preparation, and equipment logistics, just to name a few. All the while, we had to keep technology services running smoothly in the other nine school buildings. It was a test of coordination, leadership, planning, and stamina.

This chapter covers the preparation efforts during the fall semester of the 2013-2014 school year. The first half of the chapter describes the initial student laptop pilot distribution, reviews open teacher professional development efforts, and explains the PaperPlane classroom link-sharing program written by student apprentices. The second half of the chapter covers the technical details about how my team created and prepared the laptop's Linux operating system.

The Pilot Program Launch

Penn Manor High School's one-to-one laptop program pilot officially began at 8 a.m. on September 5, 2013. A small wave of students descended on the help desk. There, my IT staff and student apprentices greeted them. Any high school student enrolled in an Open Campus online course during the fall or spring semester was eligible to participate in the laptop pilot. We also offered a pilot laptop to several students with special needs. A few students declined the offer and opted to wait until the laptop program formally launched in January 2014; in all, about 90 students dropped by the help desk over the course of a few days.

The distribution of a few pilot laptops was like a small dress rehearsal before the big high school production began. We needed it. We needed an opportunity to practice. From a technical perspective, the student team and my staff could swiftly solve any support issue with ease. Learning how to work together as a harmonious support team took time. To students patiently waiting to receive their laptops, the first moments of distribution probably looked a lot like a middle school dance. Student apprentices and technology staff bumped into each other as they moved around the room. Barcode scanners got tangled. Pens and pencils had gone missing. Someone forgot to print extra bag tags. I dropped things. And paperwork was more than a little scattered. We were open for business, but a little uncoordinated. No matter—it was jubilant! Alex, Chad, and I had fun working with the student team.

Once everyone stopped stepping on each other, the distribution process was smooth. A student would arrive, present their signed laptop agreement form, and proceed to a scanning station. There, an apprentice would use a barcode scanner to scan the laptop barcode ID label into our device inventory program. The student received their accessories and moved to a 15-minute orientation, which was both a brief training and a quality control checkpoint. Before the student left the help desk, we wanted to ensure their laptop functioned properly.

Open Campus students received the trial laptop—the Acer TravelMate B113—as well as a charger, 4GB flash disk, and a bright red neoprene laptop sleeve. My team had spent the summer researching about a dozen laptops and, at the time, the Acer TravelMate emerged as the best combination of capability, price, and weight. Now we were ready to field test the hardware, and the software.

The pilot laptops initially ran the Ubermix variant of Ubuntu Linux. We preloaded a suite of free and open source software programs. The starter application list included:

> **Audacity**—An audio recorder for music and podcasting
> **Blender**—A 3D animation, modeling, and game creation suite
> **Chrome and Firefox**—Standard web browsers
> **GeoGebra**—A graphic calculator for algebra and geometry
> **GIMP**—A photo manipulation alternative to Adobe Photoshop
> **Inkscape**—A vector drawing alternative to Adobe Illustrator
> **Kazaam**—Desktop screencasting software for tutorials and videos
> **MuseScore**—A music notation program alternative to Finale
> **LibreOffice**—A replacement for Microsoft Office

OpenShot—A video editing suite
Scratch—A program to teach programming concepts
Stellarium—A sophisticated planetarium program

Students in the pilot program were spread out across the high school, not concentrated in one class or grade level. I wanted to ensure those students had a great first experience and received prompt help when technical glitches arose. I encouraged teachers to send pilot program participants directly to the help desk, no matter how trivial the problem. No appointment was needed, and drop-in visitors could walk to the help desk when they needed help. Technical support was easy to find, as the Student Help Desk apprentices and Alex were available during each class block. If a software or hardware problem would take too long to correct, they would back up the student's files, swap the problematic laptop for a new unit from our stock of spares, and restore the files to a new laptop.

Since only 90 high school students took part in the pilot program, individual feedback was critical. My team was counting on data and student recommendations to make course corrections before the main show in January 2014. One concern was that the group would use the new technology for Open Campus assignments only and not use the laptops for a wide variety of school and personal tasks. Limited student use would limit feedback and cause us to miss software or configuration bugs.

To my delight, the pilot students immediately began using the laptops for everything from schoolwork to gaming to music. Several pilot program students reported how the laptop helped them complete assignments while traveling or at home. Others were excited to have a personal laptop of their own for use at home, one they didn't have to fight siblings or parents for. A few students who didn't have access to a home computer were thrilled to gain access to the same technology as their peers.

I think our open stance toward personal music and files helped accelerate a sense of ownership. Students could connect their cameras, iPods, tablets, and accessories. My team would not provide formal tech support for personal files, but otherwise, music, pictures, and video—obtained legally, of course—were permitted, as long as students adhered to district copyright and responsible use policies.[58] Plus, students were free to install additional programs at will.

One application many students loved was Steam, the wildly popular game delivery platform from Valve Corporation.[59] Steam offered more than mindless shooting gallery games. The platform includes many challenging strategy and simulation games. Some educators may view condoning, and pre-loading, a gaming platform to be a bit anti-establishment. However, we encountered no serious classroom problems with Steam. Besides, students will always find ways to distract themselves—an online game, a passed note, flirting with the classmate in the seat behind them. Games are opportunities for informal learning and an occasional mental break.

Teacher Professional Development

Teacher support and training are critical to the success of any instructional program. In tandem with the student laptop pilot, we provided the Penn Manor High School teaching staff with as much professional development time as we could muster. Dr. Gale made time for skill development and idea sharing during faculty and department meetings. However, the core of our professional development plan consisted of three days of dedicated time for learning and preparation.

The first professional development day was an August 2013 kick-off session. Teachers participated in information and planning sessions led by Dr. Gale, the high school administration, Alex Lagunas, Shawn Canady (the school technology integration coach) and myself. On day two, faculty reworked curriculum and lessons to take advantage of the new laptops, or they practiced with the software programs.

We let teachers differentiate their professional development on the third day. Teachers could choose from two options. The first option was a traditional full day workshop. Substitute teachers covered classes while faculty attended training. This option was ideal for those who preferred a concentrated shot of technology learning.

The second, and more popular, option was akin to a choose-your-own-adventure book. Teachers were offered 20 different one-hour, after-school technology workshops and were asked to attend a minimum of six sessions. We scheduled hands-on workshops on 14 separate dates between October 2013 and April 2014. In many cases, we offered multiple topics on each date. To help with planning, we asked faculty to sign up for sessions at the beginning of October 2013. Workshop topics came from a faculty survey as well as departmental requests:

101: Student Laptop Basics—An introduction to Ubuntu Linux and the Software Center
2D Drawing and Photo Editing—Painting and drawing with GIMP and Krita software
Annotation and Document Markup—Using Xournal to annotate and markup PDF documents

Audio Recording, Music, and Podcasting—A review of Audacity, Clementine, MuseScore, and Hydrogen
Charting and Graphing—LibreOffice and Google Sheets for advanced charting and graphing
Chrome Apps—Educational tools and utilities available via the Chrome Web Store
Evernote—Help students to organize content, notes, and research
File and Resource Sharing Tricks—Techniques for sharing documents between students and teachers
Flipped Classroom Activities—Using Khan Academy and open education resources (OER) to flip instruction
Google Forms—Collect information, conduct surveys, and gather student feedback
Lessons Learned—An end-of-year session to share best practices and success stories, by department
LibreOffice—A review of the free alternative to Microsoft Office
Moodle—A review of course composition, design, and layout
Open Educational Resources—Resources from OER Commons, CK12 FlexBooks, and Open Courseware
Paperless Writing and Editing—Techniques for digital grading and feedback
Quick and Useful Web Tools—A review of useful web research tools and sites
Science and Math Program Focus—A review of programs such as KAlgebra, GeoGebra, and Stellarium
Screencasting—Turn students into teachers with Kazaam Screencaster
Student Feedback Software—Use Moodle polls and Socrative to gather student feedback
Student Blogging Basics—Getting started with authentic writing for a world audience

Teacher freedom and the flexibility to choose topics from an extensive selection of professional development options was essential to the success of the workshops. Teachers were excited to build a personalized program based on their interests and needs. The year-long format let faculty consume and digest new ideas and practices a little at a time.

A build-your-own-schedule format was not new to Penn Manor; the district offered a similar summer technology professional development model in the past. In our experience, front-loaded, one-shot conference style injections of professional development rarely induce lasting effects.

Teachers walk away with their heads spinning. However, we had never before offered so many options on so many dates. Preparing and facilitating 20 different workshops for 120 faculty members demanded epic time commitments and detailed coordination. Alex, Shawn Canady, and I initially planned to lead most of the sessions, but ultimately it became a team affair. Chad Billman, Shelby Foster, and Help Desk Specialist, Gina Kostelich, all pitched in to deliver workshops as well. Alex and I especially appreciated their assistance during the second half of the school year, once all of the students had laptops.

We held all workshops after school in the Penn Manor Library. Mixed groups of faculty from multiple academic departments attended. The bulk of the time in the workshops was hands-on. We didn't talk at teachers for an hour. To help teachers become comfortable with Ubuntu and the native applications, teachers worked on Acer laptops configured just like the student computers. For example, in my Audio and Podcasting workshop, teachers used student Linux laptops to create mini-podcast projects with the Audacity audio program and the Hydrogen drum machine program. To model our online learning software, we aggregated workshop resources, notes, and links inside a Moodle course. We encouraged teachers to chat and share ideas in the Moodle discussion forums.

Since our teachers were not running Linux on their district laptops, I offered a long-term loaner unit to any teacher who requested one.[60] Loaner laptops looked the same as the student pilot laptops. A few teachers used the loaners, but since most of the software programs covered in the workshops were available for Linux, Mac, and Windows, faculty could practice on their Mac or Windows laptops.

Starting the professional development for teachers in the fall, before the full student population received the laptops in January 2014, gave teachers substantial time to prepare and plan. Rather than cold-starting the implementation in August, at the apex of back-to-school nerves and stress, a slow phase-in approach took the pressure off teachers and promoted reflective planning opportunities.

Some educators have argued against the introduction of non-mainstream technology—Linux, in our case—to classrooms simply because the platform does not have marketplace name appeal, or because the new technology forces teachers to learn new and unfamiliar technology. This position grossly underestimates and undervalues the creativity and capabilities of teachers. In the decade before the one-to-one program, Penn Manor High School teachers had been through several computer, software, and operating system transitions. From Windows desktops to Mac laptops, faculty possessed collective experience across numerous platforms. At each transition point, district administration offered professional development and technology support. Furthermore, the varied device experiences and continuous changes prepared staff for the incoming student Linux laptops. The new laptops represented just another set of learning tools.

PaperPlane

PaperPlane took flight at Penn Manor High School in August 2013. On the first day of the one-to-one professional development workshops, Alex Lagunas introduced faculty to the new software creation of Andrew Lobos and Ben Thomas, a program destined to make typos fly away.

Alex devised the PaperPlane program idea after he noticed a frequent classroom ritual. Teachers wrote ultra-long website URLs on the blackboard. Students typed the address into Firefox and, invariably, some would get it wrong. Be it a typo or misreading, the URL wouldn't work, and the student had to look back up at the board and find the error in the string of characters. Back and forth URL checking resulted in a few minutes of lost time while everyone waited for the class to literally get on the same page.

Alex thought there had to be a more efficient way to do this. In June of 2013, he challenged Andrew and Ben to design a classroom URL sharing program as part of their summer internship work. Andrew had previously experimented with Node.js, an open source programming toolkit for creating web applications, and felt it would be suitable for the project. Ben would handle the screen layout and visual styles.

Andrew and Ben again turned to GitHub to coordinate their work. GitHub is somewhat like Wikipedia, but for programmers. Every code contribution, called a commit, is publicly open for review and evaluation. Alex could follow the duo's progress, and offer feedback as needed. Unshackled from a school day schedule, the duo hacked code throughout the summer months. On August 6, 2013, a multi-day flurry of student programming work helped PaperPlane's code reach version 1.2.[61] It was stable and ready for Penn Manor classrooms.

The system had two parts. The core of PaperPlane ran on a private web server accessible only from inside the district network. The second part was a shortcut to the PaperPlane server that appeared inside an app on the student laptops. The system worked like an embryonic instant messaging system. A teacher navigated to paperplane.pennmanor.net, entered her classroom number to create a workspace, and typed or pasted a web address. Immediately, every student laptop signed into the classroom received the URL via a little local PaperPlane desktop app—

essentially, an instance of Chrome running in kiosk mode. That was it. Web address typos disappeared like mimeograph ink in grape juice.

PaperPlane was popular with faculty from the beginning. Dianne Glock-Cornman, Agriculture Science teacher, was one of many who frequently relied on PaperPlane to maintain classroom momentum. "If we're having a discussion about something specific in class, I can zip out a URL on PaperPlane. For example, if there's an animal disease that's now starting to be an issue, we can immediately have that conversation," she said.

From a teacher's perspective, PaperPlane is an easy-to-use timesaver. It also epitomizes the power of an open learning environment in which creating a solution to a practical problem is more important than passing a test. Alex inspired Andrew and Ben with a design challenge, and they worked together to invent a whole new classroom application, one that runs on every one of the district's one-to-one student laptops. How many standardized tests have that kind of reach and impact on an entire school? How many assignments have both staff and students working together to build something new for their school?

A 40 Percent Off Technology Coupon

A few weeks into the pilot program we grew confident the Acer laptop would be our one-to-one device. Students gave positive feedback that justified our decision to use Acer laptops. After several weeks of live field testing and positive teacher reviews, I issued a purchase order for 1,725 Acer TravelMate TMB113 laptops on October 10, 2013. The cost was $313 per laptop for an 11.6" display, Intel 1.6Ghz dual-core Celeron processor, 320GB hard drive, 4GB of RAM, an Intel WirelessN card, a removable 6-cell battery, and a two-year warranty. To protect the laptop, I added a $16 padded laptop case. As a result of teacher and student suggestions, and to assist students with fine-motor skill issues, I decided to include a $5 USB mouse for every student. We also added a Penn Manor-branded USB flash drive with every kit. The laptop package cost was $339 per student, for a total hardware cost of $584,775.

Acer planned to ship the units with the Linpus Linux operating system, a free, lightweight Linux distribution designed for netbooks. There was no Microsoft Windows operating system, no Microsoft Office suite, no need for anti-virus software, and no use for commercial software management. By avoiding standard PC software programs, I conservatively estimated that we saved $200 per unit, for a total of $345,000 in software savings for the fleet. Also, use of open source graphics software—Inkscape and GIMP—as alternatives to the Adobe

Creative Suite saved an additional $15,000 in initial licensing fees. We saved $360,000 by not paying for software licenses. Put another way, the open source software community offered Penn Manor High School a special 40 percent-off technology coupon.

Course Corrections

By early October 2013, we had learned a great deal from the first weeks of the pilot. Students shared valuable, and often unfiltered, feedback. They praised the laptops as light and capable. From a technical perspective, the devices had the RAM and processor muscle to handle everything from playing music to creating videos. Students having root access to their laptops wasn't a problem. The students were respectful of the privilege and happily exploring programs on Ubuntu. They weren't cracking secret government databases.

The laptop bags, however, were not robust. I selected a slim neoprene case to help trim the kit's overall size and weight. But after a few weeks of day-to-day use by an active high school student population, the thin material already looked threadbare. It was evident we needed a tougher and more resilient carry case. But a steel case wouldn't have saved us from the first laptop damage incident. Three weeks into the program, a student dropped his laptop and cracked the screen, twice. Per our break-it, buy-it school board policy, he was billed for the damages, twice.

Ubermix, our initial operating system choice, was proving to be less than an ideal match for our pilot laptops. As a specialty-build Linux operating system for education, Ubermix was designed to make Linux as turn-key as possible for educators and schools without IT staff. Ubermix was built to work with minimal customization or technical intervention. However, our one-to-one program had unique needs that Ubermix was never designed to solve.

Our plan was to use the Ubermix distribution, tweak it for Penn Manor's program, and manage it via the district's existing Puppet software infrastructure. We quickly learned that decoding someone else's work is a time-consuming affair. Alex, Chad, and Andrew spent hours hunting down undocumented features of the operating system. Ubermix was overwriting several custom Penn Manor settings. For example, Chad was using a locally installed proxy service, called Squid, to redirect student Internet browsing to Penn Manor's web content filter. When the laptops rebooted, Ubermix reset the Squid settings, the Squid service crashed, and students were disconnected from the web filter when traveling outside of the school network. Also, Eclipse, a software development program, crashed on startup due to an undocumented change to log locations and permissions. Andrew and Nick encountered laptops with random file system errors, a problem that added to our list of troubleshooting tasks.

During our testing, application installations from the built-in Ubuntu Software Center worked as expected, but other software installations failed intermittently. Ubermix was probably designed that way so as to help guide students to a vetted software installation source. But the behavior was a problem for Penn Manor's program. With root access, our students were allowed to install software from anywhere on the Internet.

Ubermix is a terrific Linux distribution and I recommend it to colleagues seeking an entry point for Linux in schools. But in the fall of 2013, my team discovered rebuilding someone else's work for Penn Manor's needs would take more energy and time than we originally anticipated. A few weeks into the pilot, we decided to pivot to release 13.10 of Ubuntu and include Penn Manor's specific software and settings on top of it. Given our in-house Linux expertise and the existing Puppet management structure already in place in our K-8 schools, the new direction was a more viable path for Penn Manor High School.

For technical readers, the context for the decision will become apparent later in the chapter when I describe my team's DevOps practices.

On the Wrong Trackpad

To keep the software testing moving along, I requested one Acer laptop from the full order be shipped by air directly from the factory in China. The whole shipment was moving via container vessel across the Pacific Ocean and was not scheduled to arrive until the end of the calendar year. With a sample unit in hand, and a two-week head start, my team and I could finalize our golden master software image and be prepared to install it on the laptops when they arrived.

On November 26, 2013, the first Acer laptop arrived. I escorted the distinguished package to an eager high school team, where student apprentices jumped to unbox it. Selfies and celebratory photos were in order. We held the first official laptop of the main program launch. This unit would become the software mold to cast 1,724 duplicates. Alex, Chad, and the apprentices began testing our software image right away.

Glee abruptly turned to concern. The following morning, we discovered the laptop shipped with the wrong trackpad installed. Acer's sales team offered a choice of trackpad options, and the district purchase order explicitly requested Synaptic brand trackpads. However, the unit in our hands included an ELAN brand trackpad. I contacted our sales rep to report the issue and requested a review of the entire order. One wrong installation would be easy to correct, but my concern was for the entire shipment. Had all the laptops received the wrong trackpad? Our reseller contacted Acer to investigate.

A week later, we received bad news. Acer confirmed every laptop had the wrong trackpads installed. However, they had a plan. Once arriving in the U.S., the shipment would be rerouted to a manufacturing facility in California. There the ELAN trackpad parts would be removed, and the requested Synaptics trackpads installed. After the component swap, and a quality check, the entire laptop batch would be back on the road, and scheduled for delivery by December 20, just in time for the holiday break. We were back in business.

Meanwhile, I was working with Acer to acquire a proprietary trackpad software driver package from Synaptics called the Gesture Suite for Linux. The driver would unlock extra gestures on the trackpads. It wasn't essential, but it would have been nice to have the extra features. My multiple attempts to reach Synaptics to request the software for our student laptops were met with no replies. The Synaptics' company website advertised the software driver, but it was an OEM-only item. In other words, it was available to hardware manufacturers like Acer, not customers like Penn Manor.

Except, it wasn't exactly available to Acer either. Acer reached out to Synaptics but never received the Linux trackpad driver suite. Synaptics refused to make the software available to Acer, even though our laptops included a Synaptics trackpad. Further, my team's contact at Canonical, the company behind Ubuntu, was unable to acquire the trackpad software. Far from being open source, the proprietary Synaptics trackpad driver was under lock and key—and it seemed Synaptics had little interest in supporting their customers and their hardware partners.

The Software Copy Machine

Open source software is like a Lego set. You can rearrange and interconnect prefabricated bricks of source code to build an almost endless variety of new programs. As the student laptop pilot progressed, Andrew Lobos reconnected a few open source building blocks to create a software duplication machine.

Hard drive imaging is the process of automatically sending identical copies of everything contained on one laptop hard drive to hundreds or thousands of similar laptops. Imaging is a common IT practice. As you might imagine, performing the same software installation steps over and over again can be monotonous, and unnecessarily time-consuming. Several companies sell programs to make software imaging easier. One such program is Ghost, from Symantec Corporation. In Pennsylvania, academic pricing for Ghost starts around $12.25 per school computer.[62]

Penn Manor would spend more than $21,000 to license Ghost software. Of course, the open source community has developed free tools for hard drive imaging. One popular open source alternative is a program called FOG.[63] My team, and the student apprentices, had used FOG to image hard drives running Microsoft Windows for several years. It was a useful program for cloning hard drives running Windows. But in the fall of 2013, FOG wasn't suitable for imaging hard drives running Linux. The program didn't support the EXT4 filesystem language used by Linux. FOG also had a habit of scrambling the boot loader code that jumpstarts a computer when the power is switched on. You might say that FOG made our laptops give up the ghost.

The short-term solution at the beginning of the pilot program was to copy our master software image to every laptop, one-by-one, via a flash drive. Collin Enders bluntly recalled the laborious process, "We had to install everything with USB sticks. It was horrible."

Manually loading software on the 90 pilot laptops was unpleasant, but it got us through the initial pilot program launch. However, a manual copy process wasn't going to scale to 1,725 laptops. Alex and Chad had planned to investigate and troubleshoot the problems with FOG, but Andrew was keen to create a less laborious process. In fact, he wanted to build a software distribution system.

Andrew told me the idea had started about a year before the one-to-one project began. He was experimenting with software to allow his personal computers to boot from his home network. "I was playing around with PXE booting.[64] And I thought, how can I hack this device to PXE boot from my local network?" Andrew said. "So then, I wanted to build my own Linux! What's the minimal barebones thing that boots, has network and terminal support? I figured out how to build an INIT script that started a terminal and BusyBox. I did it at home on my LAN, for giggles."[65]

Drawing from his playful home experiments and frustrated by the imaging roadblocks he and the student team encountered when using FOG, Andrew began stitching together a custom imaging system from open source building blocks. His creation was called the Fast Linux Deployment Toolkit (FLDT). It resolved many technical problems:

1. Imaging used Partclone software to copy and restore only the used blocks from the file system.

2. We could copy software images to laptops via NFS or multicasted via Udpcast.
3. It ran post-image scripts, which allowed machine-specific configurations like automatically setting hostnames.
4. We could manage the imaging process via a custom Node.js powered web panel.

Curiosity, necessity, and the desire to avoid tedious labor are potent motivators. Andrew elaborated on his technical experiment: "I started on FLDT one night after FOG blew up. I was tired of working around the issues, and I realized FOG is not doing anything I can't do. So I added Partclone, an open source imaging and cloning program, to my BusyBox Linux image. And I threw together a crude web interface to manage everything."

Later, he expanded on his creation during a Reddit online discussion: "Nothing is hardware dependent. It is simply Linux PXE booted with a custom initrd. The "heart" of the imaging process is simply udp-receiver piped into Partclone. Other than that, just a bunch of shell scripts to create the separate /home partition, set the hostname, and install GRUB."

By October 2013, the student apprentices had aggressively tested Andrew's FLDT creation. It was accurate and fast. When set for multicasting to multiple laptops simultaneously, FLDT duplicated the full Ubuntu software image to a few dozen laptops in under five minutes. And after each test run, Andrew would tweak FLDT from the team's feedback and then reset the system for another test. It was beautiful to watch the student team learn through live feedback and iteration.

New features were born from the apprentice test runs and driven by a desire to spend less time handling each laptop. Andrew's post-image scripts saved lots of time. "The driving force for building features was based on need," he recalled. "I saw there was a need for auto-naming the laptops after imaging, and I added it to FLDT."

Andrew's work was an authentic, real-world learning opportunity. His efficient imaging process was used to prepare a laptop for every one of his classmates. How's that for the ultimate senior project?

As Andrew and the student apprentice team tested and refined FLDT, Chad was busy automating the student laptop software pipeline. At this juncture, our software development story gets a lot more interesting.

DevOps is Cool for Schools

Back in 2010, when the first 600 Linux laptops rolled out to elementary classrooms, my team began thinking differently about managing a fleet of computers that differed from Mac and Windows systems. In Chapter Four, I discussed how Chad led the project to adapt server management tools—Puppet and Git—to elementary classroom laptops. By the fall of 2013, his work grew into a full grown DevOps process.

But what is DevOps? Will it attack if we get too close?

DevOps is not a scary monster. It is a portmanteau of the words development (software programming) and operations (the task of keeping servers running smoothly). DevOps culture embraces collaboration between technical roles that previously operated in silos. When programmers and server administrators work together and integrate their efforts, they can release and improve software faster. It is the reason enormous websites like Facebook, Twitter, and WordPress can continuously build, test and release new features across thousands of websites, multiple times per day.

DevOps practices, and the associated open source software tools, can apply to schools as well. Security patches, system tweaks, and program updates require steady vigilance from school technology staff, no matter the devices used. When school IT staff automate routine software update tasks, they have more time for educational projects. However, our plan was unique. My team regarded the student desktop image as one big continuously evolving software program. But few public schools were using Linux on student laptops, let alone building an automated software production machine.

Penn Manor's DevOps practices may have been unique to public education, but we were no special snowflake. In the software industry, the concept of continuous delivery of new code is commonplace—the open source community solved similar problems long ago. Helpful resources, guides, and software were plentiful.

The first software tool in our one-to-one satchel was the open source Puppet project.[66] Chad introduced the Technology Team to Puppet in 2011, and by the fall of 2013, the district's Puppet framework was tested and proven. My staff used Puppet to manage security patches and software updates on elementary and middle school Linux computers. Puppet controlled every last detail of the student laptops. Network names, web browser settings, icon files, desktop backgrounds, account profiles, and software installations—all were configured inside intricate Puppet definition files. Elementary laptops were programmed to check into our Puppet servers every time they booted. If updates or changes were available, they would be automatically downloaded and applied.

Of course, second-grade student software differed from that of sixth-grade students or a middle school computer lab. To manage unique classroom needs, we developed elaborate Puppet command sets, called manifests, for grouping of student computers. When a second-grade classroom computer checked into the Puppet server, it received commands and software assigned to the second-grade group.

Given lots of unique teacher requests, the Puppet manifest files swelled and became quite sophisticated. To help detangle code hairballs, we kept the Puppet files in a server repository running Git. Funny name aside, Git is a lovely software version control system—in other words, software for organizing software code. Git's stature in software development is difficult to overstate. It is used to help manage code for the Linux kernel and Google's Android system.

Programming is like writing a screenplay, so to better understand Git, how about you and I write a movie script? Together, we sit down and sketch out a marvelous story arc for a romantic comedy. After a creative and productive planning meeting, we make two copies of the original story outline and part ways to begin writing. Our creative juices flow, but we travel two separate narrative roads. Your script is heavy on the romance; my version is a lighthearted comedy. When we meet again, the trouble begins. Each script contains memorable moments and touching scenes. But somehow, we need to combine both stories into one master screenplay. If only we had a way to merge the best parts of our stories into one blockbuster movie script!

That's where Git enters the scene. If you and I used Git to coordinate our work, we could both happily write our portions of the screenplay and, from time to time, merge our individual contributions into the master script.

The concept applies to software development. As programming teams create new code and features, individuals inevitably branch off from the main project's development road, called a trunk. As work progresses, developers "check in" changes to the software project's trunk. If you have used Google Docs to edit a document with a co-worker, you have an idea of how the process works.

Penn Manor's Puppet commands lived inside the district's Git server. When a third-grade teacher needed a new math program installed on her classroom laptops, a building technician would open the Git repository, find and change the third-grade Puppet manifest, and merge the change back into the main Puppet repository. When the third-grade classroom laptop was switched on, it would phone home for new instructions, discover the math program install command, and start the installation process.

Git was incredibly useful by itself, but with more laptops, and more tech staff working with Puppet, we needed a system for error checking and code review. One misplaced semicolon in a command file could cripple hundreds of classroom computers. Chad's solution was Gerrit,[67] an open source tool that changed my team's workflow.

Gerrit is like Wikipedia for programmers, but without the ubiquitous plea for donations. Recent code changes appear in a list of open issues. When you click on a change, both old and new code appear side by side. Code additions, changes, and deletions display in red or green.

Gerrit made software bugs easier to catch, and squash, before they caused classroom calamity. Multiple technicians could proofread tricky changes. If someone found an error, they would flag the problem, add a comment in Gerrit, and reject the proposed code change. Clean code received the blessing of a "+1" and was passed on for inclusion in the Puppet configuration.

With Puppet, Git, and Gerrit up and running, we had the infrastructure to handle the oncoming swarm of student laptops. And while Chad and my team built better IT practices, we serendipitously created unique learning opportunities for the student help desk apprentices. Gerrit was an ideal tool for teaching authentic software development techniques. Students could follow our image development process in real time. Better yet, novice student programmers could contribute in the design, development, and testing of the high school laptop image. Alex and Chad examined and reviewed student programming submissions. They merged bug-free code into the master laptop image. Code needing corrections received feedback and was sent back for additional refinement. It was an authentic design loop.

Several student apprentices participated in one-to-one laptop image programming, but Andrew was the king of code commits. He contributed 21 individual commits to the master one-to-one laptop image. Andrew made improvements to the laptops' Bluetooth behavior, refined trackpad settings, tweaked dozens of minor settings, and added software packages.

Andrew and the apprentices learned the practice of continuous software delivery, and I suspect their experience was far more satisfying than passing a pop quiz on a random collection of facts they could easily find with a Google search. What's better than opening up Gerrit and finding your code approved and merged into the master image for 1,725 peers? When we trusted our students and involved them in the development of school software, the lines between teacher and student began to blur.

Automatic for the Pupil

Our team had one more goal: to integrate every approved code change into a continuous image production pipeline. Wouldn't it be nice to have all of the bug fixes and daily software updates automatically baked into a fresh new master software image before students stepped off the morning bus? With an always current golden master image in hand, the student team could reset loaner laptops after every use, prepare laptops for new students, or recover a laptop if a student accidentally mucked it up.

Chad had the Gerrit code review system in place at the front of the image creation pipeline. Andrew's FLDT program was ready to handle imaging at the end of the line. What we needed was a process in the middle. Chad built that machinery by interconnecting several open source programs into a chain of automated tasks. Here's how it works:

1. Students and faculty test the pilot laptops. Bugs and new program requests are identified.
2. My team fixes the bug or adds new software via Puppet.
3. New code is reviewed. If the code looks good, the change is approved in Gerrit.
4. A task scheduling application, called Jenkins,[68] runs every night. It bosses around a specialized assembly program called Packer.[69]
5. Packer combines Penn Manor's custom Puppet configurations with a local copy of the Ubuntu operating system as well as Ubuntu system updates.
6. Once all of the software is fused together into one master file, known as a virtual machine image or VM. The VM image is copied to an FLDT folder.
7. FLDT copies the image to student laptops.

Chad also set up Packer to create a testing image for every configuration change pushed to Git. With intermediary testing builds, my team and the student apprentices could rapidly test a proposed software modification before including it in the master image. Most images took about an hour to build, which meant that morning code adjustments were ready for testing before the lunch staff finished baking the pizza. Some call this iterative process a fast design loop. I call it cool kids coding and collaborating in a creative classroom.

...

The laptop software image was ready, and our launch date approached. Time for Dr. Gale and I to talk with the student body.

8
High School Laptops Launch

Principal Gale and I stood at the front of Penn Manor High School's auditorium the morning of December 10, 2013. In front of us was the Penn Manor High School senior class of 2014, assembled to hear about the one-to-one laptop program. In four weeks, the program would start. We shared essential details: All students will receive a laptop, case, mouse, and USB disk. Distribution will happen in the library. Please return the signed permission forms by the due date. Personal music and files are OK so long as they are legal. Students should bring their charged laptop to class every day. No stickers on the laptops, please. Keep drinks and animals away from the laptops. Think before you write online or send an email; be kind and courteous.

But there was a deeper message. We began the assembly with an announcement: "Ladies and gentlemen, you know the laptop program is a big deal. There's a lot of adults in the room who believe the right thing to do is to trust you. And we do trust you with these devices. Sure, they're very expensive, but we know you will keep them safe. And you'll all have root access to the laptops; you'll be free to install programs and customize the software as you see fit. Most schools don't give students unrestricted access to the software on their school computers. We think it is the right thing to do, and we believe you will be respectful."

As we offered students an open world of learning, I ended my remarks with a vital directive: "Have fun, learn new things, build something amazing…be awesome!" Dozens of students chuckled and smiled. Since most teenagers are inanimate in the morning hours, the reaction was an uplifting sign.

9,128 Pounds of Open Learning

Halfway between bliss and dread, I surveyed four and a half tons of computers. The shipment arrived on 14 pallets on December 20, 2013, on the eve of the holiday break. In a few weeks, my team would prepare, process, and distribute 9,128 pounds of open source laptop learning.[70] If you've ever awoken to three feet of deep snow in your driveway, you've probably felt what I felt that day. At first, the crystal splendor of beautifully drifted snow resting below a deep blue sky is striking, almost mesmerizing. Then you realize: it's time to dig.

Before the shipment arrived, my team had reached a point where—like shoveling driveway snow—we were out of places to put boxes. The setup operation needed ample space for us to stretch out and work for a few days. At our high school, accessible, dry, and, most importantly, secure storage space has always been hard to locate. A massive shipment of laptop cases consumed the building's last suitable storage room. We couldn't commandeer teacher classrooms, so the laptop inventory and imaging phase had to happen in another school building.

I arranged to transport the laptops from the district receiving department to the Manor Middle School cafeteria during holiday break. The middle school cafeteria offered ample space, level floors for tow motors and pallet jacks, and plenty of electrical power to feed the laptops and our software imaging servers. Middle school students would need to use the cafeteria for lunch during the week, so the inventory and imaging party was scheduled to begin on the afternoon of Friday, January 3, and run through the weekend.

As the pallets arrived in the cafeteria, I grew eager for the imaging process to start. But the mountain of laptops would have to sit quietly for a little longer. The first of several January snowstorms forced us to postpone our schedule for a week.

The Great Imaging Party of 2014

As frosty plumes of January mist swirled outside, we celebrated our version of the "Stone Soup" folktale in the school cafeteria. The ingredients were: 1,725 laptops, 11 pizzas, 8 gallons of soda, dozens of cookies, free software, and a team of dedicated students driven by passion and purpose. Some schools grow vegetables in community gardens. We were cultivating collaborative student communities.

The grand imaging party commenced at 1 p.m. on Friday, January 10. As seventh-grade pupils devoured lunch and hustled out of Manor Middle School's cafeteria, we rushed in. It was time to unbox, inventory, configure, and prepare a truckload of laptops. The scheduled one-to-one distribution date—January 23—was rapidly approaching.

The Student Help Desk team of Collin Enders, Nick Joniec, Andrew Lobos, Ben Moore, and Ben Thomas joined my team. Three other Penn Manor High School seniors—Aaron Jandzio, Tom Sowers, and my daughter, Briana Reisinger—also pitched in. Gina Kostelich enlisted her son Dylan to help in the evening.

The cafeteria became a computer assembly line, a laptop imaging machine operated by my staff, student apprentices, and family volunteers. Our past experiences with orchestrating elaborate desktop PC assembly projects proved useful once again. We organized the cafeteria tables into a series of task stations and outlined a workflow process.

First, we unboxed laptops. Layers of cardboard packaging and plastic made it a laborious and repetitive chore. After an out-of-the-box inspection for shipping damage, each laptop moved to the inventory stations.

Shelby Foster, Technology Specialist, supervised the inventory stations. The crew scanned each laptop's MAC network address and serial number into an inventory control spreadsheet. Next, laptops received a Penn Manor unique barcode asset tag and a printed sticker with the device's network hostname. We recorded the numbers in another software program designed by Andrew and Ben Thomas. It was an integrated one-to-one laptop inventory and support ticket system nonchalantly titled, "Laptop Inventory and Ticket System".[71] The pair worked on it during the fall semester for their independent computer science study course.

Once added to the inventory system, the laptops moved to the FLDT software imaging station tables, supervised by Alex and Chad. There, the laptops were linked into FLDT via a network cable, imaged, and then disconnected. After a successful software imaging run, each laptop was reboxed and put back on a pallet for safe shipment to Penn Manor High School.

Alex, Chad, Gina, and I routinely worked with the student apprentices. But it was the first time other members of my staff met any of the students. When the apprentices strolled in, technicians Jason Sauders and Tom Swartz were enthusiastic, but naturally a little unsure of what to expect from the unpretentious high school students. Was Andrew's FLDT imaging system going to work? Collin laughed as he recalled the first meeting with the others: "I think it was hilarious that Jason and Tom were skeptical that we could image that many computers so quickly. I was excited to prove we could do it."

Three FLDT stations formed the heart of the laptop imaging machine. They resembled the chaotic aftermath of 1970s-era Doctor Who episodes crash landing into Jackson Pollock paintings. A computer server tower—running Andrew's FLDT software—rose from the center of each imaging station. The server pumped software into a pair of high-speed network switches. The glowing switches carried software to each connected laptop via an elaborate coil of CAT6 Ethernet cables. Power adapters and cords added to the hairball of wire, plastic, and connectors. It was a fantastic apparatus.[72]

The FLDT imaging stations were loud and swift. Steady sounds from rattling computer fans ricocheted off hard cafeteria floors and walls to create an omnipresent locomotive drone. Laptops didn't stay hitched to the noisy machine for long. Once a collection of laptops was wired in and booted into the system, software images flew out of FLDT. Even with 50 computers simultaneously connected, the engine mass-duplicated the 10GB software image to every waiting laptop in just under two minutes. Alex, Chad, and I were accustomed to the blazing performance, but Jason was stunned the first time he witnessed FLDT in action. Eyes lit up. "Wow, that was fast!" he exclaimed. Andrew and Collin grinned with delight.

Once a batch of laptops completed the imaging process, we checked each one for success or failure, and then sent the batch off for repackaging. FLDT imaging was a quick process but handling so many laptops took lots of time. Monotony set in. The work was repetitive, even in spite of a lively playlist of student selected music. By nightfall, the running joke became, "Hooray, more laptops!". Some staff and students wanted to work through the night, but I noticed the team start to fade after midnight. I decided sleep would keep everyone fresh and minimize inventory mistakes. We paused the laptop copy machine at 2 a.m. Saturday—13 hours after we begun.

After precious few hours of rest, many returned at 8 a.m. Saturday morning. Fueled by dosages of coffee and sugar, as well as breakfast pizza, we pushed onward. Little by little, we conquered the pallets of laptops. The tedium was thankfully broken by family and friends dropping in to help or deliver more snacks. My wife, Teresa, worked with Gina and Dianne Bates, our data specialist, on the unboxing and repacking of laptops. Dianne's husband Charlie and Chad's wife Jill helped keep the assembly line moving. Johnna Friedman, a school board member who headed the one-to-one committee, delivered a wickedly delicious plate of peanut butter snack cakes, which rapidly disappeared.

Hour by hour, the laptops traveled from shipping boxes to the inventory station, to the FLDT imaging stations, and back again to the pallets. You could feel the pride and enthusiasm radiating from the students. Our students owned this project; they were engaged creators, they exuded incredible passion for building the very laptop systems their peers would use in class every day. It wasn't a random class assignment devoid of meaning and purpose. It was a fellowship.

At 5:30 p.m. on Saturday, January 11, after nearly 24 hours of labor, the laptops were ready for shipment to Penn Manor High School. I was exhausted and probably a little malnourished. My feet and ankles screeched in pain from two days of near constant walking on the rigid cafeteria flooring. I needed to rest, but I didn't want the day to be over. Working side by side with the students was terrific fun. As I limped out of the now dark middle school, I had two thoughts. First, wear better shoes next time we do anything like this. Second, I had been part of a school community experience I will never forget and our students will remember for the rest of their lives. The imaging party was one of the high points of my career.

Media Attention for the Student Team

During the week after the laptop imaging party, we received an unexpected rush of media attention. I posted an article with the title "Welcome to the Laptop Machine", on the Penn Manor Technology Blog.[73] I had written about our open source stories for a couple of years, but my district technology status updates were not widely read. In fact, the site was lucky to receive 50 visits a day. That was about to change.

Our imaging story appeared on the Linux channel on Reddit, an Internet discussion and news community. The story gained immediate traction. In 24 hours nearly 3,800 global visitors arrived to read about the imaging party and district laptop program. The ensuing Reddit discussion was part technical and part encouragement for our students and our program. Andrew and members of my team answered technical questions on the discussion board. The entire Student Help Desk team received praise for their accomplishments from the online community.

Media attention didn't end there. The Linux Action Show, a popular Internet show for Linux and open source enthusiasts, featured our project on a weekly broadcast.[74] Lancaster Newspapers ran a lovely feature story on the Student Help Desk.[75] And the very same week, I was contacted for an interview with Linux.com, the website for the Linux Foundation.[76] It was beautiful to watch our apprentices receive much-deserved attention. I was proud of how the students responded during the interviews. They were a team, and no single student contributor overshadowed others on the team. Ben Thomas summed up the spirit of open source collaboration and teamwork during his interview with Lancaster Newspapers: "On this team we have a mix of people who are excellent in hardware and people who are excellent in software. We all have different talents, and we all combine them to get everything working."

Snowstorms Don't Slow Us Down

The laptops shipped to Penn Manor High School one week ahead of the program launch. We would use the intervening week to unbox and stage the laptops. Our four-day distribution plan was scheduled to begin in the high school library on January 23. But once again, Pennsylvania's unpredictable January weather scrambled our calendars. Weather-related school closures delayed the laptop launch to Monday, January 27. But in the end, the wintery weather proved useful to our schedule.

Another snowstorm forced schools and district offices to close on Tuesday, January 21. The following day, administrative offices opened mid-morning, but schools remained closed to students and teachers due to snow drifts and poor road conditions. The vacant high school building and empty library proved to be fortuitous. Once my team slid across the icy streets and glided into school, we could work with few interruptions.

Thankfully, the ice didn't stop our student technology apprentices either. Andrew, Ben Moore, Ben Thomas, Collin and Nick all traveled to Penn Manor High School to help us stay on schedule. I can assure you there was no arm twisting, bribes, or promise of extra credit. They wanted to make the one-to-one program a success. How many high school seniors do you know who would willingly give up a free vacation day to volunteer for their school? It was just how our apprentice team rolled.

In the soft library light, the incredible potential of the waiting laptop gear was staggering. As my eyes scanned the room, I was again overcome by the project's immensity. We had 1,725 of everything! Fourteen pallets of student laptops looked tiny in the vast expanse of the middle school cafeteria. But in the modest confines of the high school library, a wall of shrink-wrapped laptop pallets occluded dozens of bookshelves and choked off half the Dewey Decimal catalog.

The mass infestation of USB mice was equally formidable. We discovered each mouse individually packaged in a little cardboard box and wrapped in a plastic sheath, all of which had to be separated. And once unboxed, laptop carry cases were difficult to stack. Piled into unbalanced columns 40 high, and four dozen thick, nobody dared sneeze for fear of collapsing the whole wall into a Jenga-like tumbling finale.

As we unboxed gear, the wake of electronic flotsam and jetsam spread. Rounding the corner to the library, a brown blizzard of cardboard smacked your face. There was so much cardboard detritus that I could taste paper fiber hanging in the air. The threat of grievous, industrial-grade paper cut trauma was omnipresent.

Thursday morning we were back at it, and determined to finish unboxing the remaining 1,000 laptops. Once again, the student apprentice team willingly gave up a free snow day to help with preparations. Classes were not in session, but the faculty was onsite for a planned in-service day. Teachers who wandered into the high school library got a sneak peek at the colossal operation. Principal Gale, unfazed by the wall of equipment, pitched in to help unbox laptops.

After lunch, we took a break for an interview with Libby Clark, the digital content editor for the Linux Foundation. She read about the FLDT imaging party and wanted to talk with the student apprentices about the project and our use of Linux. We were all weary from two days of prep work, so the media call was a fun and welcome rest. Clark conducted a great interview and gave the student team a chance to open up and speak about their programming projects, apprenticeship experience, and passion for the one-to-one laptop project. Alex, Chad, and I remained as silent as possible and encouraged the student team to speak up and share their unique roles. Clark's terrific article and pictures of our setup and distribution are available on the Linux.com website.[77]

After one final frenzied push, we unboxed the last laptop, sorted the last mouse, and set up the distribution stations. We were ready to launch on the first day of the second semester: Monday, January 27, 2014. Gale, and Dr. Jason D'Amico, Penn Manor High School's Assistant Principal, had created a tight student distribution schedule, but I was confident our presorting and staging work would make the process move quickly. Distribution was planned for four days and would follow a student picture day timetable. Students would receive laptops a grade level at a time. Seniors went first, followed by juniors, sophomores on day three, and freshman on day four. Waves of students, ordered by last name, would arrive in the library every 15 minutes. Each wave included between 20 and 30 students.

Here we go!

Distribution and Transformation

The high school library was aglow with the warm light of a hundred luminescent laptop screens. Wave after wave of students scurried in to receive the open technology gift. Huddles of students and laptops and cables and bags blurred into an electric caravan stretching as far as the eye could see. The top of every bookcase became a training space. We loaded every power outlet. By the fourth day, everyone's voice was sand-blasted from the incessant repetition of the orientation training script.

The paperwork desk was a student's first stop on the laptop distribution journey. The Penn Manor one-to-one laptop agreement form granted passage. Without a signature from both the student and a parent, no student passed the paperwork station. In exchange for a completed form, the student received a pre-printed paper name tag, with the student's ID embedded in a barcode.

Next stop: The laptop assignment station. Here, students received the digital companion set to travel with them until commencement day. When a student walked up to the station, the attendant would use a barcode scanner to record the student's name tag and laptop ID numbers in Andrew and Ben's Laptop Inventory software. Refined and tested during both the fall semester program pilot and the imaging party, their software creation hummed along with minimal bugs.

Onward. Students received a laptop bag preloaded with a power adapter, USB mouse, and a 4GB USB flash drive stamped with the Penn Manor district logo. It was a practical tool and a memento for our students to keep forever. We joked how 50 years later, the students would look back at the Penn Manor flash drive and fondly reminisce about high school—and probably laugh at the ancient technology relic from the old days.

After leaving the inventory station, students stopped to slide the paper name badge into a luggage tag and then looped the name tag onto the bag. To our surprise, this was the hard part. Attaching the laptop luggage tag was a test of fine motor skill and patience. Many students had never seen a luggage tag, and they needed help manipulating the clear plastic worm loop. This little unforeseen quirk sometimes stalled the distribution caravan.

The last part of the journey was a 15-minute orientation. When students emerged from the pickup stations, they took a seat at one of the group training tables. Later, when we ran out of library tables, a long bookcase served as a flat-topped training spot. The orientation was both a checkpoint for last minute bugs, as well as a brief out-of-the-box introduction to Ubuntu. We covered a few fundamental topics and questions to get students started:

- What's in the bag?
- What are all these ports?

- How to set a local password
- A check of wireless connectivity
- A description of the Ubuntu dash and launcher
- A brief LibreOffice and PaperPlane software overview
- How to find the home folder
- Ubuntu Software Center and system updates
- How to open a support ticket
- A reminder to charge the laptop nightly

The distribution process was just as institutional as you would expect from a public school. But amid the densely packed swirl of students, in the haze of forms, bags, tags, laptops, and mice, a marvelous learning transformation was in motion. It was a day of empowerment for every Penn Manor High School student. For some teachers, we couldn't move fast enough. The fall semester laptop pilot created a powder keg of anticipation. Teachers started using the laptops for lessons as soon as students stepped foot back in the classroom.

Students were ecstatic. The afternoon of the first day, I received my first unsolicited email from grateful students: "I want to start by saying these new laptops are great so far!" wrote one. Excitement swelled in other students, many of whom never owned a laptop and never imagined they could because their family couldn't afford to purchase one. For them, it was a liberating learning gift: an opportunity to be on the same level as their classmates.

From a distance, each laptop looked entirely unremarkable with its modest black plastic shell and nondescript form. But what mattered was on the inside. Each machine carried forward the software created by passionate contributors from thousands of open source communities, all dedicated to the spirit of open sharing.

One might have mistaken our program launch as pedestrian—Penn Manor was yet another high school handing technology devices to packs of students. But we created an instructional community of practice, an open technology support team of the student, by the student, for the student. The student team was inseparable from the laptop program. We didn't flatten the classroom power hierarchy; we pulverized it.

There was no distinction between the technician, the IT director, or the student. Roles were mingled, mixed, and muddied. We had no use for assessments. Dedication and passion, not grades, drove the student apprentices. This was no contrived classroom simulation or arbitrary group project. It was purposeful collaboration and pure learning. It was design and development for real life.

Andrew, side-by-side with Alex and Chad, zipped around the library to troubleshoot bugs and answer technical questions. And at the training tables, leading the sessions, leading their peers, were our remarkable student apprentices: Collin, Nick, Ben Moore, and Ben Thomas.

There's an image frozen in my memory. In the crowded library, amid the manic cacophony, I see Nick sitting at the head of one of the training tables. Poised and serene, he's speaking to the 12 students tightly surrounding him—gesturing to a monitor, answering questions from the adults leaning in and intently listening to his every word, troubleshooting, doing authentic work, owning it, building knowledge, being the expert, being the teacher, being intense. His passion and personal connection to the school are self-evident. His self-confidence grows, his leadership skills sharpen. He is the student becoming the master. It is not only distribution day. It is his day, the student apprentice day, the day of the open classroom transformation. It is the birthday of the open schoolhouse.

9
The Power of Open

In Zen Buddhism the concept of Shoshin, or "Beginner's Mind," teaches us to approach learning with openness and a lack of preconceptions. Zen Monk and teacher Shunryu Suzuki famously wrote: "In the beginner's mind there are many possibilities, but in the expert's there are few." As we gain expertise in our work, we sometimes forget the wisdom of Shoshin and disconnect from the valuable experiences of unknowing, and the creative discovery inherent in being a novice.

Beginners must start somewhere. In formal school curriculum, learning has a beginning, a middle, and a testable end. But outside of school, learning is the result of showing up in the midst of the story and figuring things out as we go. Witness a fourth-grade student with a passion for dinosaurs. With a beginner's mind, she'll read books out of order and perhaps quickly exhaust all elementary grade-level materials before delving into dinosaur books written for higher-level students. My youthful learning passion was astronomy. I devoured everything in my elementary school library and moved on to astronomy books written for high school, college, and adult readers. I certainly didn't understand everything in those advanced volumes, but it didn't matter. Over time, I made connections even when concepts appeared out of sequence or at a reading level way over my head.

I was incredibly fortunate to have excellent public school teachers who didn't put my zeal on a shelf until I reached the appropriate age or passed a pretest. In fact, those teachers nurtured my curiosity by removing artificial learning barriers. With an unlocked laptop in hand, every Penn Manor High School student could explore and grow without limits.

Many Possibilities

By the spring of 2014, the laptops were the students' daily instructional companions. The one-to-one implementation was successful, and the new gear became a regular part of classroom routines. Outside the classroom, students learned to hack the computers to do their bidding. And the pursuit of movies and music became the mother of invention.

At the time, the Linux Spotify music service client did not have a point-and-click application install. Students could overcome that hurdle as long as they were willing to open a terminal and type a few commands. Watching a Netflix movie was more complicated. Netflix playback required the proprietary Microsoft Silverlight software plugin which was not available for Linux. To satisfy a streaming movie craving, students had to get down and gritty with the Linux command line.

One Netflix solution was Pipelight, an open source workaround for Silverlight. Pipelight required a somewhat intricate install process. Students accustomed to app store instant gratification found themselves in new territory. Another playback solution was the installation of Wine, a layer of software that mimics Windows. For many, the need for Netflix instigated a lesson on the command line and the first installation of software via the Linux APT package manager. My team took a step back and let students struggle with the process. After all, if we handed out instruction sheets, what would our high school students learn? But the effort was worth it—the installation of Netflix became a badge of technical honor.

Linux Netflix playback appeared in the Chrome web browser in October 2014. Students could browse to the website and binge on Doctor Who or Supernatural without ever touching the command line. However, extemporaneous learning germinated everywhere. Students changed more than desktop wallpapers. Alternate Linux desktop environments, such as KDE and Gnome, appeared alongside the Ubuntu Unity desktop. Screens lit up with open source CAD and drawing programs. Students created music arrangements with MuseScore and played with Blender's virtual 3D modeling clay. Fueled by curiosity, and enabled with root access, students approached the laptops with a beginner's mind. The devices became truly personal learning machines.

A few students boldly experimented with the entire operating system. One enthusiastic sophomore asked me for help when his laptop failed to boot. A river of onscreen warnings and errors gave him away, but he candidly explained his attempt to replace the school's Ubuntu operating system with Mint, an entirely different Linux distribution. As per school board policy, students were not permitted to replace the installed Ubuntu system with another version of Linux. In one corner of my school administrator brain, the policy-violation bell rang. But his intent was innocent hacking. It was playful exploration, not deliberate destruction. I blurted out, "That's awesome!" and off we went to rebuild his operating system.

Of course, not every student plunges into the command line or gets lost in programming. But the point is, they are free to do so if they choose. We trust them to make good choices, to be ethical, to be professional. We trust them to self-direct their learning. Why not let them poke around inside configuration files, or learn to setup a local Apache web server? And during the program's first two years, no students intentionally violated this trust.

Diane Glock-Cornman, Agricultural Science teacher at Penn Manor High School, believes trust and respect are integral to teaching and learning in the open schoolhouse. "Do I trust my students? Yes, because I respect them, and they know that I respect them," she says. "And I try to reinforce that environment in the classroom. And once they realize that you care enough to provide technology for them, they do take to heart that it is important, and it needs to be treated with the same kind of respect."

You'd have a hard time finding high school curriculum for Linux software installation. But if it existed, somewhere, someone would probably scrub away all of the joy and package it as a traditional linear lesson plan: "First students, we will learn the history of the Advanced Package Tool installer; please read Chapter three. Next, we'll take a quiz on vocabulary words; no, we won't use an actual command line unless we have extra time at the end of the semester. Yes class, you must submit a PowerPoint file with three facts about Linux—don't forget to include three pictures in your slide deck."

What fun would that be?

Not Like Textbooks from 1990

By the spring of 2014, the Student Technology Team was an unassuming and interwoven part of the one-to-one program. Ben Thomas recalled how his teachers encouraged his participation: "I noticed that if I said the word one-to-one, my teacher would be quick to let me out of class." Despite his unique role, Ben didn't abuse the privileges. "It wasn't like we had ultimate control over everything, we were respectful," he said. Nick Joniec added: "The help desk ran like a tight ship, like a business." Ben, Nick, and the entire student team had rightfully earned tremendous respect and admiration from Penn Manor High School's faculty and staff, but they never let it go to their heads.

Andrew Lobos was busy having fun and didn't think about his special status: "I was never like: All right, we've got the POW-ER!" he shrieked as he rubbed his hands together like a maniacal evil scientist. "It was cool because we were doing what we liked to do."

In spite of the ticking graduation countdown clock, Andrew and Ben spent the last few weeks of their senior year programming more features into the one-to-one laptop inventory software system. Their passion never waned. Three weeks before graduation, the duo raced to squash software bugs and add final touches to their creation before saying goodbye to Penn Manor High School. How many seniors are that engaged in their last days of high school?

Meanwhile, Penn Manor High School's teachers were enthusiastic about new teaching opportunities brought about by the one-to-one program. Math teacher Kim Frey said, "The laptop initiative has been the single most beneficial teaching tool afforded to me in the last 10 years of my career. I absolutely love it. I have been recording and uploading all of my lessons to a website. When the students are absent, they can watch the video of class, take notes, and do the homework. So even when they are not "in class," they can see and hear exactly what we did. And when I am absent, they just log onto their computer, and they see and hear me teaching the lesson as if I were there. It is amazing! I have had a few students that have been away for a week or so on a trip. The online videos are a life-saver for them and me."

For Emily Lyons, an English and Language Arts teacher, open source laptops became a natural extension of her instructional philosophy: "A lot of what students do is collaborative. I think I can provide the environment and the materials from which they can learn from. But once I present it, they need to work through it with each other. And 95 percent of the time I say, 'Here are your questions. Get together and work. And we'll go over the ones you don't know, or you need help with, but this is on you. You guys have to work together because that's what life is.'"

Emily observed how the Linux laptops helped detached students become more successful at writing: "I've had a fair number of kids that were traditionally disengaged—The most common complaint: 'I don't like to write, so I don't like school.' When I said, 'Well, you can type it. You don't have to write; you can type. And you can use the spell checker, and you can look up words.' All of the sudden they say, 'Oh, OK. I'll do that.'"

She also noted a change in student attitudes toward feedback: "If you're not a good writer, sitting and writing on a piece of paper is hard.

But when they have a computer that can help with spelling, and with grammar, and they can go online and look up words and the pronunciation, and they can hear how it's said, and they can write it down correctly. Now they feel good about themselves because they're not getting a paper back with a thousand red marks all over it, correcting grammar and spelling that they don't necessarily understand in the first place."

Students also appreciated the shift from traditional textbooks to digital formats. One of Emily's students shared an opinion: "I like my online textbooks because I can highlight and take notes to use at home for homework...and they are updated, not like textbooks that are from 1990."

Speaking of the 1990's, with the laptop program in place, the high school library received its first furniture layout change in nearly two decades. The original space included two computer lab areas on each end of the library, which were suddenly obsolete. We cleared away the ancient desktop computers and converted the right side of the library into a flexible learning space with eight small-group workspaces. Each workspace received laptop charging stations and a large monitor for amplifying a student laptop screen. Teachers were encouraged to schedule time in the space, even if only for a change of classroom scenery. The new configuration offered a more open, natural learning space for students to spread out and collaborate on projects.

The opportunity to redefine old learning spaces was an ancillary bonus of the laptop program, but open principles of iteration and rapid prototyping reshaped our school culture. As the laptop program developed, Dr. Gale encouraged his staff to be creative problem-solvers and to break new ground. His philosophy values experimentation, innovation, and learning from past practices. "My goal is to always be improving. I encourage teachers to try things, to take something new and run with it, and if it doesn't work, figure out why and then move forward. I want my teachers to take risks. We can become stale in what we are doing, and if we are not exploring new ways of teaching, you fall into a routine."

Emily shares Dr. Gale's drive for self-improvement and challenged her colleagues to do the same, "We ask kids to learn something new every single day. And try something outside of their comfort zone, and if, as a teacher, if you're not willing to do that yourself, then I don't know why you're a teacher."

The Open Help Desk 2.0

I've attended dozens of high school graduations, but none tied me up in knots like the June 7, 2014, Penn Manor High School Commencement Ceremony. My wife and I sat close to the ornate stage and cheered as our daughter, Briana, received her diploma. And with her, one-by-one, the inaugural student technology apprentices stepped upon the stage as well. The marching train of graduates moved swiftly. In less than 90 minutes, their high school journey had ended, and life after high school beckoned. Amidst excitement and joy, I felt a touch of loss—no longer would I randomly bump into Briana, or any of the student apprentices, while traveling the high school hallways. They had moved on.

But the graduation cycle brings new students. It brings new opportunities to work with talented apprentices eager to assist their peers with common tech issues and problems. Incoming help desk apprentices soon discover the first days of the course are a frenzied swirl of near-chaos when their summer-saturated peers arrive ready to receive laptops. There's not much time for syllabus review or introductory readings—we need to keep the laptop distribution caravan moving if we hope to get the job done in three days. With swarms of students converging to pick up laptops, new student apprentices hit the ground running and immediately begin assisting my staff. Training is live, without a net, and new student apprentices are challenged to begin immediate problem-solving and to assist with one-to-one laptop support.

Beyond laptop distribution, the Student Help Desk has evolved into a somewhat different program from that of the founding student team. For starters, it has a new home. By the summer of 2014, the help desk needed more physical storage space for equipment; it was time to relocate. The support desk moved to Classroom 200, and the vacated room became a student workroom for Open Campus online courses. The district added comfortable chairs and couches with wheels, which helped to create a friendly and relaxed learning atmosphere for focused solo study as well as group collaborative sessions.

Classroom 200 was a vast upgrade. Formally a large computer lab, the room was double the size of a typical high school classroom. My team quickly filled it with gear, and I took the opportunity to consolidate all high school technology staff and student apprentices into one common space. Our Penn Manor High School technology office was too tiny to accommodate the student apprentices. The new physical arrangement brought Alex, Chad, and Gina into the same room as the students. Student and staff workspaces were delineated, but separated by only a few feet. With everyone under one roof, collaboration between the student team and district IT staff was much easier. Imagine the space being like one part Edison's Menlo Park, one part Best Buy Service Desk, and a dash of School of Rock.[78]

During the one-to-one program's first year, Alex had worked in the same room as the technology apprentices. He was accustomed to task switching between student and staff support all day. For Gina and Chad, it was their first time in the continual day-to-day fray of the Student Help Desk. It took the team a little while to adjust to the new arrangement. Gina recalls: "It was a definite change from being in a room with just two other adults for five years. At first, I was not sure how I felt about working on a daily basis with students, but after I was able to see how the students grew and learned, it was amazing."

In time, Gina recognized the power of open classroom collaboration. "I realized what the students are experiencing, and how they interact and grow while they are here in this course cannot be taught. What they take from the Student Help Desk are real experiences that happen because they are a part of a team. The transformation for me was when I felt like the students were learning from me, learning on their own, and also teaching me."

With expanded physical space and broader supervision, we could take on more student apprentices. The student team increased to 16 new independent study students during the 2014-2015 school year and 22 students during the 2015-2016 school year. Many students joined because they loved computers. Others signed on because they were intrigued by the program and wanted to learn more. We welcomed students of all skills and academic levels. No entrance exams were needed. As long as the student loved learning and was motivated and sincere, she or he could join the team.

Today, student apprentices engage in a myriad of day-to-day support tasks. They field drop-in questions of all types, respond to student help tickets, repair laptops, manage short-term laptop loans for peers who forgot their laptops at home, and issue laptops to newly enrolled high school students. Most days are bustling with the "student customer" activity. The early morning is particularly hectic—especially on the first day back from a long weekend.

But the help desk is more than a computer repair depot dispensing digital bandages. It is a personal oasis for many students. Former help desk apprentice and 2016 graduate Brielle Bitts said, "I love working at the Student Help Desk. It is my second home to get away from everyday drama or stress. Working at the help desk with fellow students has made me grow as a person, and knowing I make a student's day when they smile or laugh about something I said is why I am in this course—and why I love it."

Student Help Desk Teams

Every student apprentice is responsible for walk-in peer technical support, but they also are part of a project team with a particular focus and function: communication, hardware, media, and programming. Apprentices are free to select a team that aligns with their interests. If a student discovers the team is not a match for their passion, they have the option to join a different team at the marking period break. The teams are:

Communications Team—The primary goal of this team is to publish new content for the one-to-one student help desk. Students manage the help desk website,[79] write and edit informational articles, and coordinate social media including Twitter and the help desk YouTube channel. Work on this team is a blend of journalism and marketing.

Hardware Team—The primary goals of this team are laptop repair accuracy, quality, and speed. Students facilitate all repairs and often perform complete laptop teardown and reassembly. They also have opportunities to experiment with mini computers and controllers like the Raspberry Pi and Arduino. The hardware team is the most popular team.

Media Team—The primary goal of this team is publishing tutorial screencasts, podcasts, and visual media for the help desk blog and YouTube channel. The students select podcast content. Topics often consist of current open source news as well as questions or tips related to the Penn Manor laptop program. Screencast tutorials cover a wide variety of software topics.

Programming Team—The primary goal of this team is learn programming and write code. Students develop software for the help desk program, student laptops, or other approved projects. My staff encourages involvement in open source software community projects. One student even participated in bug hunting for the Koha software project. The programming team usually attracts a small but focused group of students.

Penn Manor High School's master schedule includes two semesters per school year, with four daily class blocks per semester. The help desk course runs during all four blocks. Due to a practical need for help desk coverage all day, we try to schedule student apprentices uniformly into all four blocks. The result is that students are rarely together in Room 200 at the same time. Divided by time and space, it can sometimes feel like a real-world distributed team.

To encourage communication and collaboration, the apprentices and my staff congregate in a Mattermost team chat room. We host dedicated discussion channels for each student team, as well as a central "Town Hall" channel where the entire group can join in open discussion. Alex, Chad, Gina, and I monitor the chat channels and provide help and guidance when needed. Since my office is in the district office—a separate building on a different campus—the Mattermost chat space makes it much easier for me to stay in touch with the students and provide timely feedback when I'm not on-site.

Mattermost has proven to be a useful solution to the ever frustrating school change-of-class bell. It is inevitable that just when the student apprentices are deep into a project, the class bell wails, shattering the team's creative flow as everyone scampers off to another class. With the Mattermost system, our conversations continue throughout the school day, and sometimes around-the-clock. Student apprentices add ideas and thoughts from home, even over the weekend or holidays.

The Student Help Desk is like a results-only work environment. Every student is expected to maintain a regular stream of material such as technical support guides, written documentation, audio or video files, training videos, blog articles, graphics, and software programs. Teams work collaboratively, and feedback is continuous. Students are evaluated based on results, iteration of ideas, and personal projects. My mantra is: "What are you making, who reviewed it, and how can we make it better?"

Student apprentice Abigail McHenry appreciates the help desk's collaborative structure and focus on authentic projects: "I like the Student Help Desk because it allows me to learn in a worklike setting. It doesn't feel like a class, yet I feel like I'm learning more than I ever would in a strict classroom setting. It's awesome."

A Community of Learners

The Penn Manor Student Help Desk is an independent study course. Every student is challenged to create a unique and compelling personal project that breaks new ground. The choice of project is entirely up to the student. Students create software applications, write help desk guidebooks and advertising materials, code games with Scratch or Unity

3D, and produce documentary films. A couple of students even decided to write research papers on concepts like hard drive storage and PC hardware.

High school students are often reluctant writers, especially when assigned to produce work that is uninteresting and unrelated to their personal lives. However, writing is a vital part of the help desk. Apprentices, both on and off the Communication Team, regularly craft articles for the support blog. My team offers starter ideas, but the apprentices select most topics based on their interests and the support needs of their peers. In this setting, writing feels less stilted, less pedantic, and more authentic. Writing for a real-world audience is vastly different from a traditional school writing assignment where a single teacher is a sole spectator.

In January 2016, student apprentice Susan Black took her written work to a global audience. She shared her personal help desk experiences and insights in her first published article for Opensource.com (an open source community publication supported by Red Hat). Susan was the first young woman to join the Student Help Desk team. Her self-confidence and her communications skills have skyrocketed as a result of her experience supporting her peers. She writes: "I cannot imagine a more perfect day than one spent repairing laptops and solving software issues at the help desk. But being a student help desk apprentice is both an honor and a challenge. In a typical day, I collaborate with my classmates when they have technical problems and repair our school laptops. Being a tech apprentice is serious. We must update the help desk software dashboard when a problem occurs."[80]

Susan believes the Student Help Desk is more than software and hardware: "I think of our help desk room not as a class, but as a family. We motivate and teach each other, but we also have a few good laughs. We make memories daily, and I don't have to hide who I am in this class. Nobody dares to judge one another, and we become closer by our differences."

Susan's voice resonates a sense of place, a safe and inviting space untangled from the education assembly line and insulated from high school angst and drama. In this place, she is free to be herself. This is the open schoolhouse: a sanctuary at the center of a cosmopolitan community of learners.

Rewiring a Generation

When the first Student Help Desk launched in August 2013, Andrew, Ben, Collin, and Nick brought together considerable technical skill, hundreds of hours of intern experience, and uniquely tight kinship. As successive classes followed, not all student technology apprentices arrived with a robot under one arm and a home-built computer in tow. The help desk experience was the first time many students held a soldering iron, replaced a logic board, or typed into a command line.

But aren't students supposed to be technology masterminds? Surely, digital native students are computing wizards with programming skills innately wired into their synapses from birth! Right? It turns out that story is bogus. I've discovered that in spite of all the devices surrounding them, students are becoming less and less familiar with computing.

Simplified consumer gadgets sealed against digital tinkering deprive students the opportunity to explore the art and science of computing. Jailbreaking an iPhone from instructions on YouTube requires only mimic skill—there's no critical thinking or hacking prowess needed. And as technology becomes more consumerized, tinkering with the technology we own is increasingly discouraged. In the words of the Maker Manifesto, if you can't open it, you don't own it.[81]

It's easy to understand why the digital native myth becomes conflated with the illusion of computer expertise. Adults perceive rapid button pressing on a tablet as an impressive show of super technical virtuosity. And observe kids in a restaurant, on a school bus, or at a shopping mall: they're glued to their phones and tablets. All the screen time and gaming skills must translate into programming wizardry—or so it goes.

Unfortunately, locked-down, old-school practices amplify the digital native myth and exacerbate the disconnect between technology-infused learning and the act of monkeying with gadgets. Cuts to elective computer education and programming courses, often due to school budget reductions, are bad enough. But when school leadership unilaterally replaces laptops with iPads or other closed devices, they help perpetuate the indoctrination of the screen-tapping generation. Student agency and freedom are the first casualties when schools yield to tablets and wage war on computing.

I've watching the erosion of student computing skills for years. By August 2015, the scope of the problem reached a shocking level. As I worked with incoming seventh-grade students during our new middle school one-to-one laptop orientation, I saw digital natives struggle with the concept of saving a file into their home folder. Few grasped the idea of a file type or file extension. Some had problems opening and closing folder windows. The conceptual understanding of programming a computer to do one's bidding was absent. Students are a powder keg of natural curiosity. But it appears the marketing teams at Apple and Samsung have spun an exceptional yarn of enchantment. When technology is magical and polished and easy, there is no need—or option—to peer behind the wizard's drawn curtain. Corporate marketing hype would have us believe: "Why build something when there's an app for everything?"

Sealed tablets are like kryptonite for classrooms. They weaken critical thinking and a student's ability to create. Thankfully, antidotes exist. Open source software, open hardware, personal fabrication and 3D printing, programmable robots, and the implements of the maker movement offer low-cost tools to return power and control to students.

One of my goals for the Penn Manor High School Student Help Desk is to help technology apprentices discover they can command technology, and not be the result of someone else's technical or marketing decisions. Almost immediately, we ask new apprentices to dive into hands-on laptop repairs, without a safety net. Component repairs are not a simulation. Apprentices mend live laptops for real student customers. And the process is not as easy as ABC. Once the apprentice removes the outer case screws, they must grapple with a dense amalgamation of delicately interconnected circuit boards, wires, jumpers, chips, and connectors. A lot can go wrong, and there is certainly a cost associated with allowing a 16-year-old to dismantle and reassemble a laptop. But a shower of sparks can be a profound learning moment. The apprentice will realize "I cooked that logic board, now I know which wires not to cross!" After all, how can you learn to master a technique or skill without a few mistakes and meltdowns?

As one part repair desk and one part open-ended research laboratory, the help desk may look frightening to students at first. Under lighted swing-arm magnifying mirrors, an array of pliers, bits, sockets, ratchets, wire cutters, screwdrivers, screen hinges, tweezers, extractors, thermal pastes, data ribbons, screws, partially consumed laptop shells, batteries, and magnetic part trays spread out on workbenches like dental tools ready for patients.

But in time, apprentices master the tools, gain self-confidence, and cherish the experience of working with their hands to fix a broken laptop. Many students cite the repair process as one of their favorite experiences. Nick Marquette, a 2015 Penn Manor High School graduate and former help desk apprentice exuberantly said: "The help desk was one of the greatest classes offered to students. The class was like a job. I learned how to take apart the entire computer and put it back together. I was taught more than I would have learned on my own. We all learned valuable information thanks to the technology department."

My team is present as mentors and facilitators. But none of us watch over the students and tally points or grade each repair task as an absolute success or failure. We try to resist the urge to step in and do the work for the students. Sometimes we bite our lips and tense up when a new apprentice barrels in and clumsily fumbles with fragile memory chips. It takes self-control to let a student miss a repair step or forget to reattach a cable before reassembling a laptop. By allowing mistakes, and offering a supportive space to try again, we enable students to learn it is perfectly acceptable to hone their craft through practice. Iteration creates a vibrant, dynamic learning experience and puts ownership back in the hands of the apprentice. Alex states it best: "I like the idea of treating students as adults, and letting go of the idea of controlling what they are doing all the time."

We could never write a formal curriculum for the help desk. And why would we? Curriculum builds a fence around learning. There is no textbook—students simply search the Internet to discover solutions to problems, or borrow code and ideas freely shared by the open source community. They learn and play with the same support tools, software, and techniques used by industry professionals. As for testing, exactly how do you evaluate a student software project, hardware repair, or peer training session? Standard grade scales can't measure the details of a student's elation when his or her logic board repair works, or the joy of designing software used by the entire school.

What I love so much about open source philosophy, and what I strive to replicate on the help desk, is the participatory, inclusive environment where traditional power structures dissolve and students are empowered to act, contribute, express, learn, and think. Together as a team, students and staff shape the world around them. Once we stop treating students like data banks waiting for downloads, once we trust students as equal partners in their education, and once we empower students to contribute to their school community, the open schoolhouse emerges.

Students Become Builders

One morning in the fall of 2015, I was speaking with help desk apprentice, Aytekin Oldac, about course selections for the upcoming 2016-17 school year. Aytekin planned to add two AP-level courses in support of his ambition to study neurology or computing, or maybe both. He was bright and focused, and I hoped he would consider returning as a help desk apprentice during his senior year. As we prepared laptops, I asked for his thoughts about the program. The pensive young man paused for the briefest moment and added, "There is a quote from Aristotle, 'Men become builders by building.' I think that applies to the help desk."[82]

Aytekin was indeed becoming a builder. The help desk team needed a check-in registration system for students visiting the desk, so Aytekin built one. Working alongside Alex Lagunas, Aytekin set to work on a touchscreen check-in system built on top of a decommissioned point-of-sale cafeteria touchscreen terminal. Using open source LibreOffice software, he programmed a data-entry form with a big on-screen number pad. When a visiting student tapped in a student ID, the form would add a timestamp to the entry and log the visit into a database.

With no prior knowledge or instructions, he relied on his school laptop, the Internet, and his intellect to build a new contraption for his school community. The once obsolete cafeteria terminal was a laughable gray box of thick industrial plastic topped with a fry-grease resistant touchscreen. It was dull, but useful, and given a new life far removed from the lunch line.

Of course, we could have used a paper logbook for tracking help desk visitors, or rushed to the App Store to purchase a pre-made iPad registration app. But what would our young builder have learned? If there were an "app for that," Aytekin would have never spent a month studying and debugging conditional logic and learning interactive form design. He would have never prototyped a solution, decrypted sample code, squashed programming bugs, or iterated a design based on peer feedback. Empowered with freedom, trust, and open software, Aytekin became lost in the flow of discovery, hacking, and problem-solving. As a result, he unleashed an entirely new creation. I call that open, authentic learning in a high school classroom.

The Power of Open in Education

In April 2015, Elisabeth Effron and Brett Abramsky, members of the Creative Strategy + Design Team at Red Hat, reached out to discuss the possibility of collaborating on a documentary film about the high school's open source laptop program and Student Help Desk. Elisabeth and Brett discovered Penn Manor School District via my contributions to Opensource.com. They planned to launch a new film series about how openness is a catalyst for innovation and wanted to learn more about our school district. During the first planning conference call, we discussed how the high school one-to-one program evolved, as well as the philosophy of trusting students with root access to school laptops. Elisabeth inquired about specific student success stories. Ben Thomas' tale was at the top of my list.

In February 2014, after the successful launch of the one-to-one program, I introduced Ben and the other members of the student technology team to the school board at a public meeting. After well-deserved recognition from school board members, Ben's stepmother, Stephanie Thomas, asked to speak. She stood up and shared her gratitude for Penn Manor High School's technology programs. She thanked the district, the school board, and my team, but what came next was surprising and unexpected. Ben had to struggle through most of his academic career. He was a student with learning disabilities—and some had given up on him. In spite of this history, the technology program was a place for his true talents to shine.

At first, I wasn't certain I heard her words correctly. My brain couldn't process the narrative—how could the Ben I know possibly have learning issues? He was self-taught and able to program in PHP and JavaScript. He helped create a laptop inventory tracking system. He was building competitive robots. He was even taking Honors Calculus! I heard what Stephanie said about his past learning struggles, but what I had witnessed Ben create and build just didn't square with his academic history. He was an exceptional student, and his innovative work spoke for itself.

Brett and Elisabeth—as well as producer Rachel Rooney—were intrigued by Ben's transformation, and by our open source story. The team decided to visit Penn Manor High School. A few weeks later, the trio was onsite for three days of filming. The Red Hat Films crew arrived with two additional photographers, a spectacular array of film gear, and one little HD camera drone. Elisabeth told me it would be a serious production, but when I saw the bulk of lighting, camera, and sound equipment, I understood we were about to be part of a high-quality documentary.

The filming schedule was frantic. Three non-stop shooting days allowed just enough time to interview three teachers, three help desk students, Ben Thomas, his parents, Dr. Gale, and myself. Ben had just finished his first year in college and was eager to return to Penn Manor to tell his story.

Immediately after the Red Hat team arrived, the crew transformed Manor Middle School's library into a documentary set. Ben's family was interviewed first. Stephanie and Chad Thomas were open and candid about Ben's background and their frustration with a traditional academic system out of tune with his abilities. Ben was identified with learning disabilities in second grade and, later, ADHD. "He was a kid that didn't like school. He definitely struggled," Stephanie said. "But Ben was a very smart kid; he played with Legos and could build these amazing things, but they didn't see him do those things at school. We would go to parent-teacher conferences and feel deflated at the end because they just didn't see Ben for what we saw at home."

During his interview, Ben described a longstanding lack of interest in school until he found an outlet for his technology zeal. "In my freshman year, I didn't have too much of a focus. I got up and had to go to school to get through my day. But then I began to see that I'm good at this, and if I am really good at this, I want to make sure I can make a career out of it. I began focusing in school and strived to get better grades, and that reflected in my GPA."

Ben's work with Andrew Lobos and high school guidance staff on the Career Day sorting program became an inflection point: "My counselor began to realize I had more potential." His summer 2013 technology internship and the one-to-one student help desk enabled him to dream bigger and act on his aspirations. All along, he was silently overcoming his past and reinventing himself. Ben's transformation began with his passion for technology, and trust and opportunities to work on authentic programs for his school became a catalyst for his personal growth.

Ben recalled how leading four days of one-to-one laptop distribution training for his peers gave him ample public speaking practice and poise: "At first it was a little scary talking to all the students about how to use their machines. But I feel like I gained a lot of confidence talking to everyone." His father noticed a pivotal change in Ben: "Before the one-to-one help desk program, he would never have had the confidence to talk with his peers. In the program, he had to talk to groups of people. It changed his social status and his social life."

Sharing his work was also important to Ben. "Everything that I've created is on GitHub. I like to share what I make. I feel like it's important to share because I might have come up with a solution others have not found. When I was first starting and didn't know about open source, I'd be stuck on a simple problem that I didn't realize thousands of people already found a solution for. It's important to share my work with others to help them find solutions faster."

Stephanie said the student support team, and the one-to-one laptop program, was "an opportunity to showcase his talents—he didn't have that opportunity before. He never got senioritis! He got honor roll his senior year; he never got honor roll before. He worked from the beginning of his senior year to the end of his senior year—a kid that didn't like school!"

"It just changed everything for Ben. When we talk to other parents and they talk about their kid who only wants to play games and isn't interested in school, I'm like, 'Get them signed up for the one-to-one help desk; it makes a difference!'"

During the Red Hat Film interview, Elisabeth asked Ben how the student apprenticeship experience helped with his college studies. Ben, now a dual major in Computer Science and Electronic Media, replied, "My college professors definitely see that I'm a little ahead of the curve. The other students didn't have too much coding experience; they weren't exposed to open source. With the knowledge I had, I had an advantage over everyone else. One of my ideas was to develop an application that would take a template of a basic C++ structure and have it generate the file for me. When I took it to my professor and asked about ifstreams and ostreams, she was surprised I was already working at that level. I would not be where I am today without the one-to-one program."

...

The documentary Penn Manor: The Power of Open in Education premiered at Boston's Hynes Convention Center on the opening day of Red Hat Summit 2015.[83] Chad Billman and I sat close to the stage, surrounded by members of the Red Hat team. Dwarfed by the massive digital display, Thomas Cameron, Red Hat's Senior Principal Cloud Evangelist, introduced the film to thousands of Red Hat customers, partners, and community members from across the globe. I had previewed early cuts of the documentary in progress but was stunned by the final film. The gorgeous fluid cinematography; the perfect soundtrack; the passionate, and joyful student and teacher stories; Ben's moving personal story of transformation…I was overcome with emotion as I watched what felt like the culmination of a life's work unfolding on screen. I wasn't alone—there were few dry eyes in Boston that morning.

Penn Manor School District's laptop program has unlocked learning for thousands of students. But Ben Thomas' remarkable personal story shows how open principles—collaboration, participation, and trust—can build a better learning community, one student at a time.

Epilogue

The most powerful learning experience of my childhood never happened inside a classroom. It happened as part of an apprenticeship under the stars. As a child, Astronomy was my first love. I was hooked on everything related to outer space. My life goal was to obtain a Ph.D. in Astrophysics. Fortunately, before leaving Letort Elementary School, my sixth-grade teacher, Mrs. Peg McKain, helped me land the summer gig of a lifetime: an apprenticeship with the planetarium director at North Museum in Lancaster, PA. For a 12-year-old astronomer wannabe, it was like I scored a free ride on NASA's Space Shuttle.

Preparing a visual planetarium show before the advent of modern software was brutal. I learned from an excellent mentor, Dr. Jordan Marché, just how tedious the process of photographing images and building slides for planetarium projectors could be. Thinking back about these relics, they feel like some strange primitive vessels from an era today's students barely understand. Developing film the old-fashioned way offered no gratification. Working with chemicals and a mechanical enlarger, we couldn't drag a picture into a PowerPoint slide, click to resize, and reposition images on the screen. The process involved constant tinkering and trial and—mostly for me—error. It was like producing a masterwork painting with a set of broken crayons.

As my skills grew, Dr. Marché entrusted me, a gawky middle school kid, to lead several afternoon planetarium shows in his absence. Wow! I received the keys to the starship and was free to roam the open universe. At that moment, I transformed from a tag-along kid assistant to a planetarium master. It was a remarkable feeling. The experience increased my love for science and technology and instilled an appreciation for telling educational stories.

I spent three years volunteering in the planetarium, and my skills with the then state-of-the-art 35mm technology have long faded. But the feelings of trust, of being part of the team, being valued no matter my age, and of being integral to the design process of a public performance—those feelings and memories play back in high definition. Three decades later, I strive to reciprocate the agency, autonomy, and trust afforded to me as a mid-80s middle school kid. Every student deserves it.

A comet is the mascot for Penn Manor School District. I was once a student there, and I am now the Technology Director. In the winter of 1986, my 13-year-old Penn Manor middle school self, the young planetarium apprentice, caught one of the first glimpses of the fuzzy snowball that was Halley's Comet in a cold backyard mini observatory. At the time, I could have never foreseen that nearly 30 years later, my future self would hand over the laptop learning keys to 800 middle school students. When we expanded the district's open source one-to-one laptop program to middle school students in 2015, my long learning orbit had come full circle.

Halley's Comet will return to the inner solar system in 2061. What might schools be like then? Students might teleport to chemistry class or play kickball on Mars. And perhaps long before the comet's tail lights up over our planet once again, society will have changed the education conversation and designed schools to empower students.

But why wait for a cosmic sign to herald the change? We can open classrooms today. We can free students, teachers, and school leaders. We can venerate student genius and amplify their curiosity. We can say, "We trust you. We will not allow schooling to be done to you. You are an important part of your education, and you are a full participant in our learning community."

What wondrous learning will happen in your open schoolhouse?

Continue the conversation on Twitter: @OpenSchoolhouse and discover more at: http://theopenschoolhouse.com/.

Appendix: Software Resources

When selecting school software, educational merit is critical, but so is sustainability. The last thing a principal needs it to build professional development and instructional plans around software doomed to stagnate and wither on a programming vine once the developers have lost interest. Of course, the same concerns apply to commercial software. Apple, Google, Microsoft and countless others have changed pricing models and shuttered products after corporate objectives changed. And the road to educational software Hades is littered with the ashes of eager EdTech startups promising classroom miracles while ignoring their cash burn rate.

Exceptional open source software is the result of a healthy and vibrant technical community. Three stellar open source community products are the LibreOffice office suite, the Moodle learning management system, and WordPress, a web content management platform. These projects respect software freedom with an open source license. A global team of contributors committed to making the code freely available, forever. Look past the license and you can tell the software is made with love. The quality of the code and the commitment of the development communities on these three projects is incredible. Our classrooms benefit from the selfless and passionate work of tenacious programmers who have made a far-reaching impact on our students but remain strangers our students will likely never meet in person.

Free and open source software is not an all or nothing proposition. You might test a few applications at first, and add more programs once your students and staff become more comfortable with alternatives to commercial software.

For more open source school software ideas, please visit http://theopenschoolhouse.com/. Nearly all of the programs on the site are available for Linux, Mac, and Windows.

Red Hat's community site, https://opensource.com/, is another excellent resource for software ideas and success stories.

Penn Manor Code on GitHub

The Penn Manor School District Technology Team endeavors to share as much code as possible. Public schools aren't software development shops and few churn out mountains of code. But what matters is that educators participate and share their work and ideas. Schools aren't bitter corporate competitors. Why shouldn't they work together openly to create better classrooms for all students?

GitHub is a centralized service to store, share, and collaborate on software projects and programs. It is a platform for individuals and teams to create software together, and build upon each other's contributions. My team's code is available here: https://github.com/pennmanor.

GitHub may be a little overwhelming, at first. However, it is a great tool for school technology staff and high school programming courses. Newcomers will find many online tutorials, but I suggest starting with the GitHub guides themselves: https://guides.github.com.

Andrew Lobos and Ben Thomas' Career Day Sorting Program is also available on GitHub: https://github.com/4ndr3w/CareerDaySorting.

Linux Desktop Distributions

Penn Manor's Technology Team loves Linux and promotes a wide variety of distributions. However, Ubuntu is Penn Manor School District's primary student Linux distribution for three reasons. First, Ubuntu's Unity desktop interface is easy to learn. Ubuntu has a long history of polishing the desktop design to make it easy for everyday humans. Training goes fast—teachers and students are typically off and running with little more than a few minutes of orientation and guidance.

Second, millions of worldwide computers, including many large school systems both inside and outside the United States, run Ubuntu. Given the large desktop installation base, commercial software providers often support Ubuntu alongside Mac OS and Windows. For example, Logger Pro,[84] the data collection program for Vernier science data probes, is supported on Ubuntu only. Pennsylvania's Department of Education's required student assessment software, Data Recognition Corporation's DRC Insight Client, is officially supported on Ubuntu only. The DRC testing client is not unique to Pennsylvania; if your school participates in standardized testing via DRC, you can move forward with the installation of Ubuntu on student laptops as well.

Third, every two years, Ubuntu is made available as a long term support release (LTS) version. The LTS version guarantees security patches and improvements for up to five years after the release date. Long term software support commitment helps school IT staff concentrate on learning projects without constantly upgrading core system software. At the time of this writing, the current LTS version of Ubuntu is 16.04—released in April 2016. The next LTS version, 18.04, will be ready in April 2018.

Ubuntu is a project of Canonical Ltd, a U.K. company with offices worldwide: http://www.ubuntu.com/.

Your school team may also be interested in Fedora Linux, a community project sponsored by Red Hat. Fedora is an excellent Linux distribution, and the bundled Gnome desktop includes many features you won't find in Ubuntu. Fedora moves fast. Updates arrive every six months, and previous versions receive support for approximately 13 months. Discover more about Fedora at https://getfedora.org/.

Fedora and Ubuntu are two Linux flavors on a vast menu of options. DistroWatch maintains a list of trending Linux distributions: https://distrowatch.com/.

LibreOffice, LibreLearning

An office productivity suite is one of the necessities for student content creation. And LibreOffice is a wonderful toolkit for students of all ages. But too often, schools get hung up on designing curriculum around Microsoft Office. The logic is that students absolutely must learn to use Excel. If our learning goal is to have students solve problems which might happen to need a spreadsheet, the core skill is far more essential than a software name brand. Consider a spreadsheet command like "concatenate"—a function used to join two separate chunks of text into one spreadsheet cell. LibreOffice, Google Spreadsheets, and Microsoft Excel all handle the task but the steps to complete the operation differ. Why should business education teachers come to blows over which software is the best at the concatenate function? Their time is better spent helping students discover why they might use concatenate in the first place.

Unlike Microsoft Office, LibreOffice is available, without cost, on Linux, Mac, and Windows. Students and parents may install the software on their home computers. Cross-platform availability translates into a consistent experience for students as they transition from home to school. An added advantage is that parents also have the opportunity to learn the same software their child uses in the classroom. Download it here: https://www.libreoffice.org/.

LibreOffice imports and opens nearly all Microsoft Office files with a high degree of fidelity and accuracy. Like a digital Rosetta Stone, it is a handy converter and translator for many proprietary file types. This feature is especially useful in a public school, where students may bring documents created with an assortment of home computer platforms and programs.

LibreOffice is stable, dependable, and reliable. Extensive support is available via full online documentation, discussion forums, IRC, mailing lists, and Q&A sites. Even better, LibreOffice development is transparent and accessible. As an open source project, teachers and students can be participants in bug hunting, feature requests, and product development.

What if a high school student graduates and then later wants to use the files she created at college or in the workplace? When a school chooses and enforces the use of a proprietary office suite, the institution encumbers students with a potentially costly software purchase after graduation. A better approach is to offer open file format options. By supporting LibreOffice—and open document standards—we liberate our student files for life.

LibreOffice is a tremendous gift to students and educators. And the cost savings are enormous. For our school district, the educational price of Microsoft Office Standard 2016 is $45.70 per computer, per upgrade. With 4000 student computers at Penn Manor School District, the total purchase price is frightening. By choosing LibreOffice, we perpetually save $182,800 every time we decide not to buy a new version of Microsoft Office. What could your school do with those savings?

Acknowledgements

Writing a book is a community effort. A huge thank you to Scott Nesbitt, Frances Ann Squire, and Brian Wallace for development and editing expertise. Your support and recommendations took the book to a whole new level. Ellen Pollock, Phil Shapiro, and Don Watkins provided suggestions and candid feedback to improve the book as well. And thanks to Zach LeBar for his wonderful artwork and illustrations.

I would like to recognize Dr. Mike Leichliter, Dr. Phil Gale, and the Penn Manor School Board of Directors for their courage to embrace open source software and open education principles, and their drive to create exceptional learning experiences for students.

Much credit goes to the entire Penn Manor Technology Team, especially: Shawn Beard, Chad Billman, Shelby Foster, Gina Kostelich, Alex Lagunas, Jason Sauders, and Tom Swartz. I'm so proud of what you have built for our students. Thank you for your tremendous dedication, tenacity, and passion.

I want to thank Red Hat's Opensource.com and Creative Strategy + Design teams, especially: Brett Abramsky, Bryan Behrenshausen, Elisabeth Effron, Rikki Endsley, Ginny Hamilton, Jason Hibbets, Jen Wike Huger, Jeff Mackanic, and Rachel Rooney. Thank you for believing in us and sharing Penn Manor School District's open source education stories with the world. You put our students on the map.

To my colleagues in the open source software community—your time and talent made a profound difference in our classrooms. Thank you for creating the software that enables our students to create the future.

Matt Cramer introduced me to the Internet and Linux way before they were cool. Thanks for opening the door, my friend.

I would also like to thank Stanley Buch and Charles Russell, two of the finest gentlemen I've ever known.

Most of all, I would like to thank my wife, Teresa, and daughter, Briana. Your love and support mean everything to me.

About Penn Manor School District

Penn Manor School District is part of beautiful Lancaster County, Pennsylvania. Situated 90 minutes west of Philadelphia, Lancaster County has deep agricultural and historical roots. Half of Lancaster County's land is zoned for agriculture, with over 5000 farms working soil some describe as the most fertile in the United States. Lancaster Central Market, built in 1889, is the oldest continuously run farmers market in the nation. James Buchanan, the fifteenth President of the Unites States, as well as Robert Fulton, the inventor of the steamboat, were residents. During the Continental Congress' flight from Philadelphia during the American Civil War, Lancaster City became the one-day capital of the colonies on September 27, 1777.

Penn Manor's geographical boundaries encompass 113 mostly rural square miles to the east of the Susquehanna River and immediately to the west of Lancaster City. With a student population of approximately 53250 pupils, it is one of the county's largest public school systems.

Penn Manor students attend seven K-8 elementary schools, two middle schools, and one high school. Located in Millersville Borough, Penn Manor High School is directly adjacent to the campus of Millersville University. As of 2016, the district employs approximately 375 teachers and 300 support staff.

Penn Manor High School earned a Silver Medal from U.S. News & World Report in both 2015 and 2016. The high school had the highest ranking of any school in Lancaster County for 2016 and was No. 35 in Pennsylvania and No. 1,308 in the nation. The magazine evaluated more than 21,000 U.S. public high schools for the 2016 report.

Visit Penn Manor at: http://www.pennmanor.net/.

About the Author

Charlie Reisinger is a 20-year educational technology veteran. Charlie serves as the Technology Director for Penn Manor School District in Lancaster County Pennsylvania. A member of the senior leadership team, he directs instructional technology programs and technical infrastructure and operations. Charlie frequently speaks at state and national education and technology conferences and events. He is also a contributor to the opensource.com online community.

Charlie received his M.S. in Instructional Design & Technology from Philadelphia University. He is a member of the International Society for Technology Education (ISTE) and a member of the PA School Business Officials Association (PASBO). Charlie has been an adjunct instructor at Harrisburg University of Science and Technology and Philadelphia University.

Charlie is a four-time winner of the Pennsylvania School Business Officials (PASBO) Award of Achievement for excellence in school technology, and a 2009 recipient of Millersville University of Pennsylvania's Walker Center Civics Leadership Award for community Internet safety education and outreach. Under his leadership, Penn Manor received the 2011 School of Excellence in Technology Award from the Pennsylvania School Boards Association (PSBA). In March 2016, District Administration Magazine recognized Penn Manor with a Districts of Distinction Award for the open source one-to-one laptop learning program.

Follow Charlie on Twitter: @charlie3 and online at: http://www.charliereisinger.com/.

For more information about Penn Manor School District Technology initiatives and programs visit: https://technology.pennmanor.net/.

NOTES

[1] https://techcrunch.com/2016/06/07/software-is-eating-the-world-5-years-later/

[2] Dodson, Sean (August 8, 2003). "Obituary: Judith Milhon: Making the internet a feminist issue". The Guardian. p. 27.

[3] GNU stands for GNU's Not Unix! GNU's design is like the Unix operating system.

[4] https://www.gnu.org/gnu/manifesto.en.html

[5] https://www.gnu.org/philosophy/free-sw.en.html

[6] http://www.telegraph.co.uk/technology/2016/08/06/the-worlds-first-website-went-online-25-years-ago-today/

[7] The original Internet discussion boards.

[8] USENET is no longer maintained. The original message is archived on: https://groups.google.com/forum/#!original/comp.os.minix/dlNtH7RRrGA/SwRavCzVE7gJ

[9] http://www.cio.com/article/3069529/linux/linux-is-the-largest-software-development-project-on-the-planet-greg-kroah-hartman.html

[10] http://www.linuxfoundation.org/news-media/announcements/2015/02/linux-foundation-releases-linux-development-report

[11] http://www.pasbo.org/AOA

[12] Moodle.org logs user profile creation dates. I'm proud to have one of the oldest accounts!

[13] Usage stats via Moodle.com.

[14] https://w3techs.com/technologies/details/cm-wordpress/all/all

[15] https://wordpress.org/about/license/

[16] https://wordpress.org/plugins/

[17] http://www.penspra.org/CommunicationsContestWinners.aspx

NOTES

[18] http://www.pennpoints.net/2010/10/22/penn-manors-online-newspaper-had-a-fantastic-first-year/

[19] http://studentpress.org/nspa/awards/2010-nspa-online-pacemaker-winners/

[20] Yes, Teresa is my wife.

[21] For reference, a popular LMS, Schoology, is currently priced at $5 per student, per year.

[22] Pricing is compared to proprietary services such as Schoolwires.

[23] Estimated pricing for Follett Destiny support.

[24] Whitehurst, J. The open organization: Igniting passion and performance. (Boston: Harvard Business Review Press, 2015), 17.

[25] https://freenode.net/

[26] Slack pricing and terms as of August 2016: https://get.slack.help/hc/en-us/articles/206646877-Slack-for-Education

[27] http://www.mattermost.org/

[28] The code is here: https://github.com/pennmanor/

[29] http://www.crn.com/news/networking/229100302/hp-hangs-up-on-3com-voip-vars.htm

[30] http://www.sipxcom.org/

[31] We initially used ownCloud. The Nextcloud project is a fork of that software. https://nextcloud.com/

[32] See: http://io9.gizmodo.com/5974468/the-most-common-cognitive-biases-that-prevent-you-from-being-rational

[33] https://thejournal.com/Articles/2010/07/15/How-To-Get-Started-with-Open-Source-in-K-12.aspx

[34] https://thejournal.com/Articles/2012/03/07/Building-21st-Century-Writers.aspx

NOTES

[35] https://insights.ubuntu.com/2010/03/13/andalusia-deploys-220000-ubuntu-desktops-in-schools-throughout-the-region/

[36] Flowchart for app procurement: http://www.zdnet.com/i/story/62/16/001376/ios-volume-program.jpg

[37] Google announced the Chromebook laptop in May 2011.

[38] https://www.gnome.org/

[39] http://www.xfce.org/

[40] https://puppetlabs.com/puppet/puppet-open-source

[41] https://git-scm.com/

[42] The stories of early school laptop programs are detailed in the book Never Mind the Laptops: Kids, Computers, and the Transformation of Learning by Bob Johnstone.

[43] http://www.wired.com/2010/04/apple-scratch-app/

[44] Pennsylvania testing software is supplied by Data Recognition Corporation: https://pa.drcedirect.com/

[45] http://www.ubermix.org/

[46] Papert, S. *Mindstorms: Children, Computers, and Powerful Ideas* (New York: Basic Books, 1980), 5.

[47] The FAQ and other one-to-one documents can be found here: http://technology.pennmanor.net/.

[48] Freire, P. (2000). Pedagogy of the oppressed (30th anniversary ed., p. 72). New York, NY: Continuum.

[49] *Ibid.*, 76.

[50] PHP is an open source scripting language for web development.

[51] The Arduino is an open-source hardware kit for controlling physical devices.

[52] Technology Student Association, a not-for-profit for STEM education.

NOTES

[53] https://github.com/

[54] For Inspiration and Recognition of Science and Technology: A U.S. charity that designs programs to motivate young people to pursue education and careers in science, technology, engineering, and math (STEM).

[55] https://getbootstrap.com/

[56] Radio-frequency identification (RFID) chips are used to identify and track objects, and pets.

[57] https://www.gnucash.org/

[58] See http://technology.pennmanor.net for the policy documents.

[59] http://www.valvesoftware.com/

[60] At the time, proprietary software requirements prevented us from upgrading teacher laptops to Linux.

[61] https://github.com/pennmanor/PaperPlane/

[62] Pricing as of September 2016: http://www.iu13.org/administrators/statewide-software-sales/

[63] https://fogproject.org/

[64] Pronounced like Pixie, the mythological creature. The Preboot eXecution Environment is software to boot a computer.

[65] LAN: Local Area Network - A network inside a school building or home.

[66] https://puppetlabs.com/puppet/puppet-open-source

[67] https://www.gerritcodereview.com/

[68] https://jenkins.io/

[69] https://www.packer.io/

[70] 4,104 Kilograms: Stamped on the shipping bill.

[71] The original system: https://github.com/pennmanor/LaptopsandTickets-1-1

NOTES

[72] For photos, see: http://technology.pennmanor.net/2014/01/15/welcome-to-the-laptop-machine/

[73] http://technology.pennmanor.net/2014/01/15/welcome-to-the-laptop-machine/

[74] http://www.jupiterbroadcasting.com/49842/hdr-photography-on-linux-lass30e06

[75] http://lancasteronline.com/news/penn-manor-students-help-classmates-get-tech-savvy/article_87e46ad2-0553-55bd-a49b-3b86cbf888e2.html

[76] https://www.linux.com/

[77] https://www.linux.com/news/featured-blogs/200-libby-clark/761499-pennsylvania-high-school-rolls-out-1700-linux-laptops-to-students

[78] A musical comedy film: https://en.wikipedia.org/wiki/School_of_Rock

[79] Visit the Student Help Desk site here: http://blogs.pennmanor.net/1to1/

[80] https://opensource.com/education/16/1/getting-started-in-it-through-a-student-run-help-desk

[81] http://archive.makezine.com/04/ownyourown/

[82] From the Nicomachean Ethics - http://classics.mit.edu/Aristotle/nicomachaen.2.ii.html

[83] Watch the film: https://www.redhat.com/en/open-source/stories/penn-manor

[84] See: http://www.vernier.com/downloads/logger-pro-linux/

Made in the USA
San Bernardino, CA
10 August 2017